Lakeland Fells

75p

Other Dalesman books on Lakeland:

EARY SETTLEMENT IN THE LAKE COUNTIES
FAMOUS LAKELAND HOMES
GEOLOGICAL EXCURSIONS IN LAKELAND
GHOSTS OF THE LAKE COUNTIES
GRASMERE AND THE WORDSWORTHS
A HISTORY OF CUMBRIA
THE JOHN PEEL STORY
LAKELAND BIRDS
LAKELAND COOKERY
LAKELAND GEOLOGY
LAKELAND MAMMALS
LEGENDS OF THE LAKE COUNTIES
MINING IN THE LAKE COUNTIES
THE NATIONAL TRUST IN THE LAKE DISTRICT
RAILWAYS OF THE LAKE COUNTIES
WALKING IN LAKELAND (3 volumes)

Lakeland Fells

by
Frank Goddard

DALESMAN BOOKS
1975

The Dalesman Publishing Company Ltd.,
Clapham (via Lancaster), North Yorkshire

First published 1975

ISBN: 0 85206 295 8

Printed by Galava Printing Company Limited, Hallam Road.
Nelson, Lancashire.

Contents

Introduction   7

1. Coniston
   The Old Man of Coniston—Dow Crag—Wetherlam
   —Swirl How   9

2. Langdale
   Blea Rigg — Langdale Pikes — Pike o' Blisco —
   Crinkle Crags—Bowfell   13

3. Grasmere
   Loughrigg — Fairfield — Steel Fell — Calf Crag —
   Gibson Knott—Helm Crag   18

4. Troutbeck
   Wansfell — Yoke — Ill Bell — Froswick — Thornthwaite Crag—Caudale Moor   22

5. Longsleddale
   Grey Crag — Tarn Crag — Kentmere Pike —
   Shipman Knotts   26

6. Mardale
   Harter Fell — Mardale Ill Bell — High Street —
   Kidsty Pike   30

7. Ullswater
   Loadpot Hill—Bonscale Pike—Hallin Fell—Place
   Fell—Helvellyn   37

8. Keswick
   The Caldbeck Fells—Blencathra—Skiddaw   42

9. Coledale
   Causey Pike — Eel Crag — Wandope — Hopegill
   Head—Grisedale Pike   47

10. Borrowdale
    Grange Fell   Rosthwaite Fell — Glaramara —
    High Spy—Catbells   50

11. Buttermere
    Grasmoor—Whiteless Pike—Red Pike—High Stile
    —High Crag—Haystacks   58

12. Ennerdale
    Great Borne — Haycock — Steeple — Scoat Fell —
    Pillar   62

13. Wasdale
    The Screes—Great Gable—The Scafells   66

The cover photographs show:— Front: The Langdale Pikes from the Blea Tarn road; Back: Great Gable as seen from Lingmell. All uncredited photographs, including the covers, are by Tom Parker. Other photographs were supplied as follows:— Derek Widdicombe, page 33; G. V. Berry, 35; R. Ellwood, 53 bottom; C. H. Wood, 55 bottom; P. Walshaw, 56 bottom.

Introduction

THIS small book is not intended as a guide to walks. There are others which more than adequately cater for such a need. Its purpose is to introduce the Lakeland fells to walkers new to the region and perhaps provide the basis of reminiscence for those familiar with the ground. By no means all the fells find space within these pages. Only brief mention is made of the Dodds north of Helvellyn; the central fells between Thirlmere and Borrowdale are omitted; certain individual fells of great character have no place—Fleetwith Pike and Eskdale's Harter Fell, for example; and most of the delightful minor hills are regretted absentees. Those fells included, however, form a useful cross-section. They are conveniently grouped by valley, village, town or lake, moving in an anti-clockwise direction round the district, finishing at Wasdale partly because that dale means more to me than any other and partly because the high hills of Wasdale are the obvious climax to the Lakeland fells as a whole.

On reading through my typescript I feel I may have given an underlying impression that perhaps the fells have too many visitors. This will certainly seem to be the case to anyone walking on the more popular heights in mid-season. It has been suggested that possibly a thousand visitors may tread Helvellyn's summit on a sunny summer bank holiday and this is by no means an exaggeration. The real point is that there are many areas that remain quiet even at these times and I have tried to show where such peace may be found—but not to the extent of revealing all of Lakeland's backwaters. There are places where the walker has a fair chance of remaining undisturbed which are not mentioned in this book, but with the aid of a map and a little initiative anyone can find them for himself. Out of season the tourist high spots too can be unfrequented. I have enjoyed walks in relative solitude even on Scafell Pike and Helvellyn by choosing my time well—and in glorious weather. If we can syphon off only a few of those who usually make for the better known attractions at busy times then Cumbria will still have room for the increasing transient population that will inevitably come this way.

Lakeland is as well provided for in literary output as any region of Britain—more so than most. Perhaps this small book will whet the appetites of those who read it and lead them to writers whose specialist works make a minor library of information and interest that is a constant source of pleasure for walkers absent from the fells.

1.   Coniston

The Old Man of Coniston—Dow Crag—Wetherlam—Swirl How.

WHEN John Ruskin elected to make his home at Brantwood, on the eastern shore of Coniston Water, he chose well. The view across the lake looks into the heart of the Coniston Fells from just the right distance for a realistic appraisal. Here is a compactly fashioned group of hills with a high skyline connecting all the main summits. Hanging from that challenging ridge is a series of splendid coves, a large scale sculpture forming some of the finest rock scenery in the Lake District.

In the vanguard of this grand array is the Old Man of Coniston, peering possessively down to the village at its toes. This must be one of the most visited fells in the district, but it has received the attentions of man since long before the first tourists came on the scene. Miners have quarried their way almost to the summit —indeed they have left their mark on all the hills of this group. The Old Man could well be called the Industrial Archaeologist's Mountain for there is much to examine among the ruins and rusted artifacts resting by the wayside. The desolation of Coppermines Valley in particular holds a fascination for those whose interest lies in this direction. Even now industrial mankind has not finished with the fell. Explorers are likely to be disturbed by the detonation of explosives as yet more of Coniston's venerable guardian is removed for sale to a stone-hungry world.

The summit is a regular promenade, an important port of call for all able-bodied visitors to Coniston. The stones of the large slate plinth that crowns the highest reaches are so well established as to seem a natural extension of the mountain. This platform and its environs support lesser cairns of much more ephemeral existence. The feeling is that some visitors, unable to build sandcastles as in their more normal holiday habitat, seek solace in the production of stone substitutes. A tourist tide removes their efforts, only to rebuild with equally transitory towers. This is a game common to all popular summits but here it seems more evident, perhaps due to the plentiful supply of useful sized building material.

Nevertheless, Coniston Old Man is a good mountain to climb and despite its popularity anyone with the patience to study a map can find quiet ways about its flanks. I have wandered undisturbed down the south ridge when the route by Low Water certainly had its usual quota of determined pedestrians. The fell was long held to be 2,633 feet high, though an old and battered Ordnance Survey map of mine clearly affirms its height to be 2,635 feet. My latest map disputes both these figures, giving the altitude as 2,631 feet. Perhaps all those tourists are wearing the Old Man away but it retains its pre-eminence as the highest in he group—by just one foot.

This area is an exceedingly rich one for "tarn baggers". including that in Little Langdale there are seven major tarns, some of which have seen service as reservoirs. Perhaps the best is that which lies due west of Coniston Old Man: Goat's Water. This is usually considered as part of the Dow Crag scene and properly so for it is an essential component of the best approach to that fell. The dominating buttresses of any crag look their best with a foreground of water and this situation is one of the finest of all.

Dow Crag has been a favourite with rock climbers since the earliest days of the sport, but it also has much to offer the fell-walker. A direct ascent from Goat's Water is quite obviously ruled out, though a scramblers' route is to be found at the south end of the main face. This traverses diagonally to the left but adventurers in the region should turn back if confronted by a definite rock pitch. They are certainly on the wrong route. The safest ways to the top are from the Walna Scar Pass, or from Goat's Hause at the head of Goat's Water's cove. Select the latter for preference to enjoy the excitements of some superbly rocky architecture from a position of security. If combined with an approach from Torver or Little Arrow this gives a splendid outing with the dramatic outline of Dow Crag growing more impressive all the way.

Viewed from the west, from the valley of the Duddon, Dow Crag is hardly worth a second glance but its summit is that of a mountain in the truest sense. The bones of the fell reach for the sky and achievement in attaining the top is synonymous with the satisfaction of scaling a real peak, a feeling enhanced by the nearness of the profound plunge that terminates in the barren scree slope that is the western shore of the tarn.

Dow Crag and the Old Man mark the limits of Lakeland's high fells in this direction and they are the shop window of the Coniston Fells. However it is the ridge system of this group that makes it such a satisfying area for walkers. Possibly the best way to gain a general knowledge of the group as an inte-grated unit is to follow the ridge from Wetherlam round to the

Old Man. This is the main skyline as viewed from the east bank of Coniston Water and is an excellent day's expedition.

The best way to start the walk is by way of Tilberthwaite Gill. Access to the ravine was once made easy by a series of wooden catwalks and steps. That was a time when genteel tourists felt they had a duty to visit places endowed with the manifestations of Romantic scenery. As the popularity of this sort of thing increased Tilberthwaite Gill deservedly enjoyed the attentions of a large influx of trippers and this pedestrian way gave pleasure to a great many folk. Now the wooden walkways have perished and present day walkers must make do with tracks on either side of the gill. When the destination is Wetherlam the true left bank holds the better choice.

The Tilberthwaite area is riddled with mines and quarries. Indeed there is one at the outset, but walkers leaving the head of the gill are well advised to keep their eyes open and their wits about them. A particularly hair-raising form of Russian roulette could be played here by any fellwalker, tired of life and equipped with a blindfold. Warnings of dangers inherent in old workings have often appeared in print. I make no apology for repeating them. The mines were perilous enough when in use and claimed the lives of countless miners. Their state after years of disuse and neglect can well be imagined. The only sane advice is: Keep Out!

The Wetherlam track rounds the misleadingly named Dry Cove Moss to reach the skyline below Wetherlam Edge. We once reached this point as mist manoeuvered mysteriously around from the Greenburn side of the fell to meet us at the ridge, where a line of cairns is a useful pointer to the summit in such conditions. An occasional glimpse down to the Greenburn valley gave us a tremendous sense of isolation and added greatly to the stature of Wetherlam's final pyramid. The west ridge is much more extensive than might be expected from a casual glance at the map. It is by no means impossible to go astray here in mist but if reasonable care is taken Swirl Hause will soon be underfoot. This is a fine col, not much used as a pass, but frequently by walkers en route for Wetherlam or Swirl How, whether they have come up from Coniston or Little Langdale, or are doing the Coniston Round. There is no mistaking the place. It forms a neat break in the ridge and is one of those spots that linger in the memory.

On a quiet day of the year, when the main throng of pedestrians is absent, this is a good place at which to pause. It is far enough away from the evidences of civilisation to be imbued with the remoteness of far hills and you can sit near the cairn and let your eyes take in the surrounding scene. Typical of mountain Lakeland, these heights are imposing and make no

11

concession to those short in wind and frail of limb, at least until the ridge is reached. Otherwise they make concessions to no one at all—more than one aircraft has come to grief hereabouts. There is wreckage less than a mile away on Great Carrs and to the south, down by Levers Water, the undercarriage of another plane has found a final resting place. When I last passed that way its stainless metal gleamed brightly (it is not by the beaten track) as though the tragedy had occurred only the day before.

The way from the col is up a rocky ridge with the somewhat forbidding title of Prison Band. Do not let the name put you off. It is a good way for scramblers and leads directly to the summit of Swirl How. Perhaps the going is getting rather worse here for, as on other well used routes, the constant pounding of boots is producing an unpleasant form of scree that has nothing to do with the normal eroding properties of seasonal weather changes.

Swirl How must qualify as the prince of these Coniston Fells. Its very name has a ring of remoteness and mystery and the accepted summit is superbly poised above the head of the Greenburn valley, just where Prison Band climbs up from the depths. I have never been there on a sunny day. For ever in my mind this is a place of drifting mists or of sparkling frost, ice and snow. But it thrives on such conditions. This is a place for the lone walker, in a way that Coniston Old Man can never be. The plateau to the north and south shows the bedrock of the fell here and there, and the summit cairn has an apron of grey stone. Maybe Swirl How fails to be the highest of these hills by a solitary foot but let no man deny it the right of sovereignty over its satellites. Sitting at the geographical centre of its attendant fells, it is the lord of all it surveys.

2. Langdale

Blea Rigg — Langdale Pikes — Pike o'Blisco — Crinkle Crags — Bowfell.

GREAT Langdale has long been established as one of the Lake District's most popular fellwalking valleys. Roads from the expanding conurbations of Yorkshire and Lancashire converge on long suffering Ambleside from where it is the obvious magnet. A disappointment to many tourists is the lack of a lake, though the flat valley floor above Chapel Stile probably contained one before an accumulation of silt resulted in its disappearance in prehistoric times. A lake would be a natural consequence of glacial activity, and the wealth of crags that makes this such a popular rock climbing centre is certainly due to the action of ice.

The valley's northern boundary between Chapel Stile and the Langdale Pikes rises to the widespread ridge of Blea Rigg. Like much of the country in the immediate neighbourhood this is a hill of many summits, and jagged decorations of crag overlook the flanking valleys. A pleasant track wends a devious way from hollow to hollow en route to higher land in the west. There are tarns, small but cheerful pools. The largest seems to be Lang Howe Tarn. It has a number of alternative names, all quite justifiable, but as Lang Howe is a nearby knoll this title is suitable enough for me. As you approach from the east you come upon it suddenly on rounding a small upthrust of land. The tarn is quite shallow and tends to become overgrown in summer, but if the weather is right this can add charm to the scene and its placid, reedy waters form an excellent foreground to the distant challenge of the Langdale Pikes.

The Pikes have one of the best recognised mountain profiles in England and their ascent is a must for anyone enjoying a first visit to Langdale. Though only of modest height they contain within a tightly circumscribed area more excitement than many an entire valley. If you wish to taste the flavour of real mountains with a modicum of effort this is the place to go. The number of pikes is variously held to be from two to five but any argument on the subject is of little consequence. It is sufficient to realise that all candidates are worth a visit and the opportunities for exploration endless. Unfortunately the capacity of such a compact group to accept visitors has limits and in season they are limits often passed. In fact there are few days when you can wander alone upon tracks that have been beaten beyond endurance by an inestimable multitude of boots. The way up the west bank of Mill Gill to Stickle Tarn is now so worn that it is hardly a pleasure to tread.

However, Stickle Tarn occupies so splendid a position that it is easy to understand why this way has enjoyed such attention. Here is a display to rival that of Dow Crag and Goat's Water. It may be that Dow is a better crag from the rock climber's point of view but scenically the combination of Stickle Tarn and Pavey Ark is the more effective. The crag, larger than anything in this group, always appears dark to me. Its physical presence almost reaches across the water to command the walker's attention as he emerges from the confines of Mill Gill. The tarn, poised at the lip of the ravine, is restrained by the wall of weathered stones that forms the dam built some hundred years ago in connection with the defunct gunpowder works at Elterwater. Water powered the machinery and the tarn was a useful reservoir to compensate the varying flow of Langdale Beck. Visually the dam has little effect as a despoiler of the scene. In fact its presence is an asset, for when you stand by the inlet stream the eye sails smoothly across the waters to the distant hills of Coniston with a negligible rim impossibly preventing a catastrophic flooding of the valley between.

Behind Pavey Ark is Thunacar Knott, an undistinguished high point on the broad expanse of land coming down from High Raise, a fell which has some claim to being the most central in the Lake District. Stand anywhere on this plateau and you have little indication of the thrillingly buttressed façade presented to viewers in Langdale. Only Pike o'Stickle gives evidence of what lies beyond, protruding above its hinterland like a big toe through a hole in a sock. Its small summit is a fine place from which to view the simple lines of the upper Langdale valley, where Mickleden terminates in the trough end of Rossett Crag. From the Pike there is an uninterrupted plunge of nearly 2,000 feet. Not far below is one of the many stone axe sites found in recent years in the immediate area.

The most distinctive crag on this fellside is Gimmer, which rises to a summit at Loft Crag. As you travel up the valley this tends to hide Pike o'Stickle and together with Harrison Stickle provides the outline that quickens the pulse of both walker and

14

climber. Perhaps the best vantage point for an appreciation of the sheer quantity of these mountain delights is the car park near the New Dungeon Ghyll Hotel. How many folks have hastened to pull on their boots at this spot with eyes held aloft to the enticing tumble of grandeur surrounding the widely carved ravine of Mill Gill? There can be no better place to start a day in the hills, with such variety of rock displayed in so small a compass.

Across the valley is an exciting mini-pike that figures well in the Langdale scene. Though merely half the height of its illustrious cousins over the way, an incident on the west ridge of Lingmoor Fell, Side Pike is well worth a visit—but remember that the only safe line of ascent or descent is on the west. Taken in combination with an exploration of its parent fell it presents an excellent outing when the popular fells have their full quota of visitors.

Lingmoor's western neighbour is Pike o'Blisco. It has an abundance of those features that make a hill into a mountain in every sense of the word. Apart from mere steepness there should be plenty of crags in evidence, streams should descend by deep gills abounding in waterfalls and a distinct summit— preferably reached by a rocky scramble—should be well in view from the valley. All these features has Pike o'Blisco and, what is more, it can lay part claim to two major tarns apart from a couple of tiny ones indisputably its own. Blea Tarn is the fell's most famous water but Red Tarn has a more remote situation and there is greater satisfaction in reaching a spot where picnic trippers have no place.

One of the attributes of Pike o'Blisco is the variety of routes to the summit, including one for lazy walkers who are not ashamed to take a car to the top of Wrynose Pass. Even so there is still over a thousand feet of ascent to be accounted for when using this back door, and a number of interesting features can be linked together to make a pleasant afternoon on the heights. A route taking in Black Crag, with its miniature "Napes Needle", has merit, and after a gentle exploration of the environs of the summit a return by way of Red Tarn makes an enjoyable outing for anyone willing to leave the car behind for a couple of hours.

But to enjoy the best of the mountain the ascent should be made from valley level. Probably the most popular track is that to Red Tarn, diverging from the highway up The Band at Stool End Farm. Alternatively, the path from the Blea Tarn road above Wall End Farm and leading into Redacre Gill has much to offer, especially on a hot day when the proximity of cool, running water has undeniable attractions. A combination of these two walks, best done in an anti-clockwise direction to have the view of Langdale ahead on the way down, makes an excellent round.

15

The summit of Pike o'Blisco is a gem. There are two tops with a little gully between. On the highest point is a fine specimen of a cairn, though it does not quite boast the excellent proportions it once had. Some years ago it suffered at the hands of those whose misguided pleasure it was to push the upper half to the ground. More thoughtful visitors have since rebuilt, almost to the original specification. With or without its cairn, this is a place at which to linger. Pike o'Blisco pushes its rocky spine beyond a thin skin of turf into the highland air and provides the satisfied climber with hard but adequate couches on which to recline after enjoying the view.

The track down to Red Tarn continues west, by-passing Cold Pike and swinging north to reach the ridge of Crinkle Crags. For those who like to walk on high, with plenty of rock on hand and a little scrambling to add spice to the proceedings, there is nothing quite like this crenellated skyline in Lakeland. To most folk Crinkle Crags **is** the ridge, despite the scope for working out stimulating routes on all flanks. It is a mountain of many tops (or Crinkles), each a worthy enough summit to grace any fell, but the highest point is sufficiently pre-eminent to prevent challenge. It extends westward as the rough declining spur of Long Top, giving this 2,816 foot peak some standing as the true focal point of the mountain. The main axis, however, follows a north/south line and forms a superb link between Pike o'Blisco and Langdale's premier mountain, Bowfell.

My first sortie on Bowfell occurred when two of us had a small tent pitched in Mickleden (at a time when such free camping was not banned in the National Park). With a singular lack of subtlety we stepped straight on the mountain from our tent and forced our way directly up a juniper entangled gully to emerge black and breathless on The Band. Here the royal road from Langdale was joined, a route that remains a classic in the fellwalker's itinerary.

Really, there is only this one popular track on Bowfell and it continues beyond the summit to the col of Ore Gap where a bed of tiny and colourful pebbles crunches crisply underfoot. Most visitors use this route, with possibly such variations as the traverse below Flat Crags to the foot of Cambridge Crag. That is an airy and rewarding track for it introduces walkers to the great crags of Bowfell and there is a splendid sense of space in the unremitting plunge of fellside that sweeps down to Mickleden. A further benefit is to be found at the foot of Cambridge Crag where a sparkling spring awaits to fuel the final drive to the top, usually made on the east side of this dominating bastion of vertical rock.

Of course there are other ways up the mountain but they need more initiative. Bowfell is quite a distance from other valleys—

not too far for a seasoned walker but requiring a conscious effort when other good things are nearer to hand. I remember an approach over Rosthwaite Fell, Glaramara and Esk Pike, returning to Borrowdale down Langstrath. It was a long but enjoyable day with as its climax one more visit to the rock-strewn pyramid that crowns one of Lakeland's giants.

3. Grasmere

GRASMERE is such an admirably situated village that there can be real problems in deciding on a route for a day's walking in the fells. So much that is worthwhile is available on all sides that only those who can manage an extended stay, or a frequent return, can fully enjoy the manifold delights of the area.

Of the smaller fells Loughrigg is supreme. Here is Lakeland in miniature; the many diminutive streams, valleys, tarns, crags and summits are a Lilliputian mountain system which forms a perfect introduction to the district as a whole for any newcomer with ideas of taking up fellwalking. Loughrigg is a happy fell which in summer throngs with cheerful family groups. There is ample scope for minor exploration and it is by no means impossible to go astray amid these devious acres. Access is available on all flanks so this is not exclusively a Grasmere fell, though it does figure largely in the ring of hills that encircles this fair vale. It is linked on the west with Silver Howe, another eminence that enjoys an affinity with Grasmere. These are foothills of the central mountain spine of Lakeland, quite as accessible from here as from other valleys around its periphery.

Across the lake is the western fringe of the system of ridges rising to Fairfield, one of Cumbria's major fells. It is Grasmere's misfortune that ascents from this side fail to show the best of the Fairfield group. There is no doubt that some of the most dramatic and exciting of mountain scenery is there for the entertainment of the discerning walker but Fairfield's crags are revealed only on an approach from Patterdale. Perhaps the finest walk is a circuit of Deepdale by way of Gavel Pike and St. Sunday Crag, returning over Hart Crag and Hartsop above How. Nevertheless, one classic round demands the attention of Grasmere based walkers: the Fairfield Horseshoe. It is a walk that few pedestrians omit from their itinerary early in a fellwalking career.

There is, however, one outing that only Grasmere can claim as its own. This is the circuit of Greenburn, the ridge from Steel Fell to Helm Crag passing over Calf Crag and Gibson Knott. It is not a long walk. The average walker could complete it in a short afternoon but such race-track tactics would hardly do justice to a delightful little horseshoe. Here is a route of contrasts. Helm Crag can be guaranteed its quota of tourists on most days of the year but the other extremity of the circuit is a most satisfactory objective which you can often have to yourself.

Steel Fell is the hill which presents such an unpromising front to travellers whose eyes turn west on a crossing of Dunmail Raise. From there it has little to offer, but it does project an air of character from the road east of Grasmere. Regrettably it is overshadowed by the closer proximity of Helm Crag, which is a pity because an ascent by the south-east ridge is very agreeable indeed. A highlight for me is the delightful little zig-zag where the track negotiates a tiny outcrop some two thirds of the way up. It comes at just the right point to break the possible monotony of a naturally straight line to the summit from the enclosures above Gill Foot.

The ultimate point is marked by a reasonable cairn but the fell's best known heap of stones lies a thousand feet below on Dunmail Raise. That massive, unshapely pile, now marooned on the central reservation of the new double carriageway, is for non-walkers probably the most famous cairn in Lakeland. It is popularly supposed to indicate the grave of the last king of ancient Cumbria but, though it is likely that Dunmail was involved in a battle with the Saxons hereabouts in 945 A.D., he afterwards made his way to join an ally in Wales.

About a mile along Steel Fell's west ridge is a shallow, 100 yard long stretch of water nestling in a peaty depression with a few attendant tarnlets as company. Prior to 1966 Steel Fell Tarn was not shown on the one inch O.S. map nor, I believe, on any other map of the district—a fact noted by W. Heaton Cooper in **The Tarns of Lakeland** and A. Wainwright in his **Pictorial Guide** (Book 3). It would be satisfying to assume that at least one employee of the Ordnance Survey has been prompted by the comments of these eminent writers to do something about the omission. The tarn is now clearly marked though it remains un-named.

The dale on the northern side of the ridge is that of the Wythburn, though it does not largely figure in the view unless you go out of your way to observe it. The head of Wythburn valley is known as "The Bog". More than likely this is an old tarn bed, as is the case with Greenburn Bottom at the head of the adjacent valley. The wetness of Wythburn reaches up to the ridge at the dale head, where there can be problems in rounding

19

the upper reaches of Greenburn's valley to reach Calf Crag—unless you perversely prefer spongy rather than springy turf beneath your boots. The watershed here is imperceptible and really the term "ridge" is quite ambitious.

Calf Crag is a good place for a break. The summit occupies a position near the edge of a wall of rock. Careful pedestrians can select a ledge near the cairn where, with toes dangling in space, a quiet lunch can be enjoyed. Below one's feet is the head of Far Easedale with its track leading over Greenup Edge into Borrowdale. The view in this direction is not extensive but is the most satisfactory, although to the east there is interest in picking out the various summits along the watershed of Fairfield, Helvellyn and the Dodds. In prospect is the crinkly little ridge leading back to Grasmere.

Along here the agility and speed of that mountain prince, the sheep dog, was once brought vividly to my notice. I was looking down to Greenburn and noticed a shepherd surveying the fellside from a point near the beck. His dog was by his side. As I was taking out my pipe the dog set off up the hill in my direction and before I could load and light the battered briar it was by my side. With a friendly wag of the tail it pushed a wet, investigatory nose into my hand and, evidently deciding that my brand of tobacco was inedible, turned and sped back to the valley as abruptly as it had come. I was left with the impression that I had been momentarily mistaken for a particularly ragged old sheep overlooked in the last gather and experienced a sense of relief in being spared the attentions of the local shearing expert. Nevertheless I took the hint and visited my barber at the earliest opportunity.

Gibson Knott is the last summit before Helm Crag. It is worth pausing here if only to take a look at the overpopulated final eminence ahead. Prudent walkers will time their arrival at the most popular top on the walk so that the busiest part of the day is over when they get there. So many folk do of course know Helm Crag better as "The Lion and the Lamb". Its short summit ridge bristles with rocks which assume a variety of shapes as seen from the A591 road as it passes through the vale of Grasmere and up Dunmail Raise. It is because of this natural sculpture that the fell has been labelled "the best known hill in England". If you wish to climb to the highest point you will have surmounted one of its set pieces, that at the north-western end of its two hundred yard long top. Whether you will then be standing upon the Lion and the Lamb, the Old Lady at the Organ or the Howitzer depends upon the point of view from the busy road below.

There is another Lion and Lamb, the "official" one, at the other end of the miniature ridge. This is the one seen from

Grasmere and is the O.S. station, given the height of 1,299 feet —not as high as the other group of rocks but easier of access. Between the two Lions is a bewildering tumble of stones in a couple of pronounced grooves that are well known to all who have been up there. It is a place to which can be devoted a couple of hours of thorough exploration; time well spent on a sunny afternoon.

4. Troutbeck

Wansfell — Yoke — Ill Bell — Froswick — Thornthwaite Crag —Caudale Moor.

THE fells surrounding the pleasant valley of Troutbeck are well in view from the busy Kendal to Ambleside road and a high density of traffic also passes up the dale bound for Ullswater and Helvellyn. The vale seems more open than most. Its confining slopes are relatively gentle and its mouth is wide, looking out across Windermere to the tree bedecked undulations of Claife Heights. Troutbeck may not erupt with the excitements of a Striding Edge but its flanks attract an appreciative band of wanderers to their grassy rooftops.

To the west is Wansfell, though it owes more to the patronage of Ambleside based walkers who usually make the short climb from Stock Ghyll. The hill is a less satisfactory objective from Troutbeck when considered as a competitor to the ridge across the valley but Wansfell Pike rewards visitors with a fine outlook over Windermere. It is not the topmost point for there is higher ground a mile or so to the north-west, but this is not as satisfying a goal as the Pike. Circumscribed by tussocky hummocks and crossed by walls, it has little merit as a point of vantage and is only sought out by pedantic peak-baggers. For most folk the Pike marks the limit of exploration on Wansfell.

The ridge east of Troutbeck rises from modest foothills between Staveley and Windermere but the first true summit is nearly five miles north of such gentle beginnings. This is Yoke. Though there are more stimulating things to come you can enjoy the real flavour of the fells in its ascent. The hill has a special place in my memories because one wild winter's day south of the top I came closer to a wild red deer than I have ever been in my life. Battling against a tremendous gale, in the lee of a wall whose shelter was mainly the product of a fertile imagination, I peered over its stonework and found myself face to face with a fine stag. It is difficult to say which of us was the more startled yet there is no doubt about which came to his senses the first. With a cursory snort of annoyance the creature turned on its heels and melted into the encircling mist, leaving me with the impression of having seen a ghost.

The Kentmere side of Yoke is where the main interest lies. There the rocky framework of the ridge is frequently exposed and the fierce plunge of Rainsborrow Crag makes any suggestion of a direct ascent from that valley unthinkable. From the east this is every inch a mountain, a complete contrast to the commonplace slopes presented to those travellers bound for Kirkstone and beyond. In fact it reaches its peak north of the valley proper, due east of the minor hill that plugs the head of the dale—Troutbeck Tongue.

The mountain which most captures the attentions of those who linger in the vale of Troutbeck is Ill Bell. It can probably lay greater claim to being Troutbeck's fell than any other. Bell by name and bell by nature, it needs no vivid imagination to realise the aptness of the name. If a section could be removed from the ridge at its highest point, like a slice from a cut loaf, the outline of a bell would be obvious. It would be a bell with a super-abundance of handles, however, for this fell is crowned by more than its fair share of cairns. They sprout from the summit like quills on a hedgehog's back. There is no mistaking Ill Bell. It has a namesake a couple of miles away to the north-east but that it the one needing to be qualified by the addition of the parent valley's name to its title. Mardale Ill Bell is a worthwhile hill yet the mountain above Troutbeck is the one we refer to when we talk of Ill Bell.

The general rule for Troutbeck is of smooth slopes and easy ridges, on the other side of which any crags are to be found. Perhaps this is what prompted the Romans to start their High Street here, for that high level route began its push for the tops on the eastern side of the valley head. The grassy groove may seem almost an accident of nature, some minor landslip, until you stand some distance away and view it as a whole. Nature does not provide such a well graded route for the use of human beings.

The Roman road builders engineered as easy a way as they could for the travellers of their day, though perhaps the Romans were not the first regularly to cross these hills. The early Britons did have long distance tracks before Caesar stepped on our shores. There are ancient ways across the Pennines and elsewhere of proven antiquity, along which Celtic and pre-Celtic remains have been found, including stone axes from Langdale. I can visualise the pre-historic artisans of that valley despatching their wares over these fells in their quest for trade. Whoever first designed the route, it has been well used in post-Roman times—and before the advent of fellwalking. The Troutbeck section is named Scot Rake on some maps and no doubt plundering tribes from across the border found it to their advantage. The old pele tower of Kentmere Hall is a witness to such troubles of days gone by. Shepherds too would find this a useful way on to the High Street range.

Scot Rake is on the slopes of Froswick where it has been adapted by modern foot travellers. Froswick appears as a smaller replica of its southern neighbour, Ill Bell, in some views. This is particularly noticeable from the direction of Mardale Ill Bell. It has a pleasant little summit but is really no more than an incident in a grand ridge walk. This is not a place at which to pause for long. It is too close to better things to command such attention. An obvious target for many a walker is the fifteen foot beacon on Thornthwaite Crag, which is well in view from the valley and must invite interested comment from visitors there. Perhaps it is as well that not as many of them are attracted this way as to the more positive magnets of the district. Outstanding cairns elsewhere have been destroyed by thoughtless vandals. The examples of Pike o'Blisco and the famous memorial of Robinson's Cairn on Pillar immediately come to mind. No one would like to see the Thornthwaite Beacon suffer a like fate.

West of Thornthwaite Crag, effectively separating it from Caudale Moor, are the depths of Threshthwaite Mouth. This is a definite col between Troutbeck's upper valley and Threshthwaite Glen. A pedestrian here is standing within some hundred yards of headwaters that eventually find their ways into England's two largest lakes. Windermere and Ullswater are eight miles apart in direct line but should you choose to journey from one to the other by following the watercourses that almost meet at Threshthwaite Mouth the mileage would be considerably greater. This would be an interesting proposition for any walker whose appetite for the peaks is at an ebb.

The most massive fell of the group that encloses Troutbeck is Caudale Moor. It throws out an extensive system of ridges, including the one that marks the western limits of the valley, rising to Wansfell and its Pike before dipping its toes in Windermere some six miles from the summit. Caudale Moor is alternatively known as John Bell's Banner and sometimes Stony Cove Pike, though this last name should only be applied to the summit. It is a misleading title. Do not go up there expecting to find a peak as provided by the pikes of Langdale. Caudale Moor's highest reaches take the form of a wide plateau and though maps credit the fell with an altitude only two feet above 2,500, those two feet must be represented by a relatively large area on the ground.

Caudale Moor is one of those fells seen by countless thousands of Lakeland's visitors but arousing little comment, despite the fact that the road they travel impinges upon the western flank. Mostly travellers heading south from Ullswater have eyes only for the "Kirk Stone" and Lakeland's highest inn, and northbound tourists have Brotherswater and Patterdale in view. It must be admitted that this aspect of Caudale Moor offers little competition. Nevertheless, the initiated few will realise that behind the dull façade is a mountain of great character and those who choose to venture upon it will find full justification in their choice.

5.   Longsleddale

Grey Crag—Tarn Crag—Kentmere Pike—Shipman Knotts.

IT is some five miles from the inconspicuous turning off the A6 to the limit of Longsleddale's metalled road at Sadgill. For the fellwalker, however, these five miles are but a prelude. For him the best of the valley is the final couple of miles beyond the hamlet, where the road gives way to an old quarry track. From here to the head of the dale at Gatesgarth Pass the landscape is formed from rocks of the Borrowdale Volcanic series with, for much of the way, all the implications of Romantic grandeur faithfully realised. The lower section of the valley is carved out of shales, grits and slates—a different type of country altogether, though by no means unattractive. Between these two areas is a very narrow band of Coniston Limestone. Judged by its bedrock Longsleddale is a vale of great variety.

Such judgement is borne out by intelligent observation. The dale begins to take shape at Garnett Bridge, just off the A6. The lower valley is not deep but it is steep sided in true glacial fashion. Deciduous woodlands help to colour this pastoral land a rich green in summer and at the close of the year the place glows in a riot of autumn hues. Always the river Sprint maintains its unifying thread through old lacustrine basins and short gorges on its way to join the Kent a couple of miles north of Kendal.

This land is not without interest to walkers but the walking is not such as will appeal to the single-minded devotee of the fells. Not until he arrives at Sadgill will his eyes begin to glow with excitement for only then do the flanking slopes reach for the 2,000 feet contour. This is good ridge-walking country and there is no better introduction to the heights of the upper valley than a horseshoe circuit of these fells, starting and finishing where the road ends. For me it is a circuit best done in an anti-clockwise direction, if only because a reverse tour would result in a final section directed away from Lakeland and that is too sad to contemplate. Though the head of the valley is inescapably a Lake District scene there is revealed beyond the eastern rim

26

something quite different, in fact a Pennine upland. While such terrain can provide excellent walking country its flavour is alien to the Lakeland hills.

Grey Crag is the first port of call. An ascent could be made from the side valley of Stockdale but, though this aims more directly for the summit, it lacks views of Longsleddale Head. I prefer to face the more immediate steepness of the south-west ridge which has minor excitements to relieve any monotony. There are small outcrops, and a breach in the first tiny crag involves the passage of a few feet of scree. The opportunity to pass one's hands over bare rock always enlivens the day. Once Great Howe is reached, after the second wall, all gradients are gentle.

Those who look out for it will see, slightly downslope on the right, an unusual structure overlooking Stockdale. A detour for closer examination does little to alleviate curiosity but a study of the one inch O.S. map is an aid to comprehension. To find the word "cairn", in plain lettering rather than that used to represent antiquities, is sufficiently rare to be of note. In a land where cairns, as the walker understands the term, must be numbered in their thousands this seems a surprising circumstance until you consider that their multiplicity mitigates against official recognition within the confines of a one inch to the mile scale. (The $2\frac{1}{2}$ inch map does acknowledge the presence of the more permanent examples, but with the more prosaic title "pile of stones".)

In the area under discussion the word occurs four times, and therefore one might reasonably expect to find something unusual at the site. One of these cairns is genuine enough, being the beacon above the scattered stones that rejoice in the name of Artle Crag. If a ruler is placed against the dots denoting the positions of the other three it will be found that a straight line through the points can be produced to a further dot in Haweswater, labelled "Twr". This is the pump tower of Manchester's reservoir and a clue to the purpose of the structure on Great Howe. It is one of a series of survey posts built by Manchester's waterworks engineers during the construction of the aqueduct that carries Lakeland's water out of the district. The survey stations, their function long completed, now stand forlorn. They seem to emphasize the loneliness of these infrequently trodden hills.

Grey Crag owns a summit whose lack of obvious features causes it to fade soon from the memory. More easily remembered is the depression that must be crossed en route for Tarn Crag. Here an area of marsh and peat hags lends uncertainty to progress. Even after a dry spell we once had to contend with a short stretch of thick, black mire. An inquiring stone, large and weighty, vanished with an obscene belch and we moved on quickly, thankful that our feet had been placed with care. Away to the Longsleddale side of the ridge fence is Greycrag Tarn, hardly distinguishable from the general morass. Its existence is largely a matter of history, recorded only on maps.

Tarn Crag presents a defiantly rocky face to Longsleddale, glaring across to the equally uncompromising abruptness where Goat Scar defends Kentmere Pike. Buckbarrow Crag helps to build a scene to challenge most that Lakeland has to offer, but elsewhere Tarn Crag is generally tame. Its most unusual feature is the second of the survey posts. This is a tower of huge proportions, fifteen or more feet in height and of considerable girth. Littered around are ageing timbers that once formed a platform to make the business end more accessible for the surveyors. This peculiar piece of architecture, with its distinctive notch at the top, puts to shame the tiny cairn that marks the fell's highest point, some two hundred yards to the east.

Lack of notable features would make it easy to lose your way on these peaty tops were it not for the fence, and even this by-passes Tarn Crag's summit. It is a sure guide to the depression which connects the head of Longsleddale with remote Mosedale, where is recorded one of the loneliest bridleways on the Tourist Map. Beyond the Mosedale pass rises Selside Brow culminating in the summit of Branstree, properly a fell of Mardale though it does lie exactly at the head of Longsleddale. We once spent a pleasurable half-hour observing a small herd of red deer grazing across this slope. These hills are lonely enough to appeal to such shy animals and there is provender in plenty to satisfy Fell ponies too, when they choose to roam this way. Upper Longsleddale is quiet enough now, though it once rang to the sounds of industry. There are old quarries low on the flank of Branstree. Other workings in Wren Gill, below Harter Fell, are much more extensive and should be treated with caution. This is a place especially to avoid when mist is a threat.

Harter Fell, like Branstree, is better considered as a Mardale mountain but it is unavoidable on this circuit and is the best hill on the route. It follows the pattern of the preceding fells in having a namesake elsewhere in Cumbria. I suspect that many will consider the counterparts to be better fells. Gray Crag (Hayeswater) and Tarn Crag (Easedale) may well be so, but in the case of Harter Fell it is only the Eskdale fell's summit that can really claim superiority. Certainly the northern aspect of its Mardale cousin, with its combination of tarn and rock scenery, is as good as anything in the district.

A fence keeps to the height of land all the way round to Brown Howe where it joins company with a substantial wall that gives fair protection in windy weather on the approach to Kentmere

Pike. When reached this seems to be no pike at all. The main excitements of the hill are concentrated lower down on the Longsleddale side and are best appreciated from that valley. A more satisfactory summit is that of the subsidiary, Shipman Knotts, the final eminence on the ridge south before it loses identity in the sprawling open fell beyond the Kentmere/Sadgill track. Centrally placed on that grassy wilderness, and well in view as you head that way, is the tarn of Skeggles Water.

The descent from the rocky bumps that mark the upper limits of Shipman Knotts commences by way of a pleasant, elongated hollow. Minor outcrops cause deviations in the track, which continues until it joins the Kentmere/Sadgill pass. This occurs more or less on the band of Coniston Limestone, evidence of which can be noted in contributions to local walls. The way down to Longsleddale ends below Sadgill Wood, possibly a relict woodland of Lakeland. If so, it is quite in keeping with the nature of the valley. It is a place seemingly overlooked by time, where the ancient pele tower of Ubarrow Hall is a forgotten sentinel of days gone by.

6.   Mardale

THE grand array of fells overlooking the head of Mardale can readily be climbed from other valleys and such is often the case. The journey to Mardale is long for anyone based in the popular centres of Lakeland. This is a pity for these are mountains of great contrast whose west facing slopes are generally dull, but they display rugged grandeur to Haweswater's valley. All ascents from there of necessity have the same starting point: the small car park at the end of the long and lonely road. The fact that this lies at almost 900 feet means that in terms of mere height these are among the easiest high fells in the district.

Harter Fell has some claim to being Mardale's premier mountain, rivalling even High Street as an attractive proposition for walkers. It thrusts a façade of crag and corrie towards the valley and takes under its wing two outstanding natural features. There is no better example of corrie tarn than Small Water and the climb out of this rocky basin brings the superb col of Nan Bield Pass under foot. Walkers passing this way enjoy scenery without equal in kind anywhere in the National Park. I have memories of coming down from the heights, after days of glorious summer weather, to rest beside this delectable mountain lake and watch the shadows of evening play upon the backcloth of crag and scree. The track above aims steeply for the skyline to slip through a notch in the true tradition of all great mountain passes. The whole situation is so like the volcanic craters of imagination that it is almost a disappointment to realise that this scene was sculpted by ice, not fire.

Nan Bield Pass connects with Kentmere where the initial descent traces a series of zig-zags that add piquancy to the upper reaches of this highland trail. Here are the western limits of Harter Fell. The eastern extremity is likewise bounded by a well known pass, that of Gatescarth. The northern face between these two routes is scarred by plunging crags, in every way characteristic of the best in Lakeland. In view of such circumstances one almost feels cheated to find on the top a rounded, grassy pasture with no suggestion of the drama so near at hand. A new fence follows the watershed, replacing one that has for long years been practically non-existent except as cairn fodder on the fell's summit. The addition of iron posts has given an eccentric appearance to this signpost of the hills and I have come to expect even more extravagant composition in metal-work on each successive visit.

Mardale Ill Bell, often dismissed as a shoulder of the High Street range, lies west of Harter Fell. Fashioned in the same mould as all these hills, it shows its most craggy face to Haweswater. Perhaps of less merit than its neighbour, it does score in one respect. Scramblers can enjoy mildly sporting routes in stirring surroundings from the foot of either Small Water or Blea Water. Harter Fell's rocky front is for looking at, not for climbing. Mardale Ill Bell is most usually visited as one incident in a round of the Mardale tops. Its grassy summit holds little to inspire the seeker of mountain splendour except as a viewpoint for the ridge of Troutbeck's Ill Bell, seen here to advantage with pyramid peaks etched sharply against the sky.

Highest of the Mardale group—in fact the loftiest land east of Kirkstone—is High Street. Though the name is usually given to the mountain there is the feeling that properly it should be applied to the range as a whole. After all, the title is derived from the high level route used by the Romans to connect their forts at Ambleside and Brougham. The Roman way does not visit the highest point but passes some hundred yards to the west, near the edge of the steep Hayeswater flank. The wide, flat summit has been a meeting place for the dalesmen in the more recent past. Here they escaped the confines of the adjacent valleys to find an ideal arena for sporting pastimes and the sounds of racing, wrestling and revelry rang out in the rarified air. Now the thud of galloping hooves and falling bodies is no more. Only the gentle plod of the fellwalker's boots shares with the sheep the freedom of these high places.

High Street is the climax of the longest continuous ridge in this fell country, a route that cuts right across the district in an almost straight line from north to south. It is the best part of twenty miles from Pooley Bridge to Troutbeck, a splendid traverse for the long striding fellwalker. These are easy miles to cover, the gradients gentle, and between the extreme summits of Loadpot Hill and Yoke there is no point below the 2,000 foot contour. In these days of car-based walkers the route enjoys less popularity than it deserves for no one likes to finish the day a score of miles from his personal transport. I suppose the answer is to leave the car at one end and use public transport to reach the distant starting point, or to do the walk in partnership with friends who are willing to exchange ignition keys on passing. Otherwise the Roman way is best considered as part of a walking tour that takes one progressively round the district. These days this proposition is one that few other than Youth Hostellers consider.

Though it is common practice to climb High Street from other valleys, notably Troutbeck and Patterdale, the finest way up is from Mardale. Here is the classically direct lateral ridge of Rough Crag and Long Stile, with a shallow tarn in the minor depression between the two. The hollow, Caspel Gate, is sometimes wrongly called Gospel Gate, probably by walkers with a biblical turn of mind. Those with a working knowledge of Lakeland terminology will be familiar with the use of "gate" to denote a low point on a ridge. It is almost synonymous with "pass", so disappointment is in store for folk who expect to find a man-made obstacle in their way. The depression can hardly be called a pass either, for the ridge separates two remote mountain recesses, Riggindale and the cove of Blea Water. Only a shepherd could have reason to use it as a short cut between the valleys. Still, it is a good place for walkers to gain the ridge if they wish to include a visit to Blea Water in their itinerary, though this means that the pleasures of the preliminary approach over Rough Crag are missed.

Blea Water has attractions, however. Its greatest claim to fame is its depth for, at 207 feet, this is the deepest tarn. Of the lakes only the two W's—Wastwater and Windermere—are definitely deeper, with Ullswater as a possible third. All this lies hidden beneath the surface, but what is visible is impressive enough. This is a wild, remote water set among crags. The only regret is the proximity of Small Water, forever its superior in all but size and depth.

As the ridge of High Street continues north it passes over Rampsgill Head and High Raise before ceasing to owe allegiance to Mardale. Neither of these has the power to excite those who scale the heights from this direction, but the former sports a subsidiary summit to catch the attention on an approach to the valley. This is Kidsty Pike, the most notable peak in the area when viewed from the distant east. It is doubtful whether anyone would ever make Kidsty Pike the sole target of the day. More likely it will be treated as a bonus on a visit to neighbouring tops. The cairn stands at the brink of the precipitous declivity overlooking Riggindale, an airy situation indeed, but the other side has an easy gradient. This sudden transition from gentle slope to abrupt crag makes the outline that gives the fell its claim to the title "pike". It is a dramatic enough finale to the notable circle of fells ringing the head of Mardale.

32

The Old Man of Coniston viewed from Machell Coppice, on the east side of Coniston Water (chapter 1).

The Langdale Pikes and Great Langdale in winter guise (chapter 2).

Froswick and Ill Bell from St. Ravens Edge (chapter 4).

Harter Fell from the southern end of Haweswater. The Gatescarth Pass
to Longsleddale is to the left of the mountain and the Nan Bield Pass
to Kentmere to the right (chapter 6).

Fell ponies near Nan Bield Pass at the head of Kentmere (chapter 6).

7.   Ullswater

Loadpot Hill — Bonscale Pike — Hallin Fell — Place Fell — Helvellyn.

PERHAPS the finest approach to any mountain region is by boat. Impetuous youth, anxious to get to grips with the fells, may disagree but there are times when I can think of no better way to the charms of Lakeland than by sailing up one of England's major lakes with a vista of hills gradually unfolding ahead. Ullswater presents a perfect setting for such self-indulgence. From the gentle foothills around Pooley Bridge there develops a minor voyage of discovery amid a wealth of sylvan beauty. The upper reaches of the lake have a fine mountain backdrop of Romantic grandeur with deep, mysterious valleys reaching into the heart of a highland hinterland.

These fells, Helvellyn and company, are the ones that most readily come to mind when planning walks in the area but there are many other heights, quieter and more remote, available for those who care to seek them out. Such is Loadpot Hill, placidly resting on the north-eastern periphery of Lakeland. It offers little in the way of dramatically exciting scenery but still exerts a peculiar attraction all its own. The summit occupies a position where the northern foothills of the High Street range begin to converge, and the fell takes under its wing a number of satellites which hold a great deal of individual character.

The Romans knew the place for their road from Ambleside to Brougham passed west of the summit. Students of Roman history have investigated the authenticity of this route by digging out a section on the northern approach to Loadpot Hill. Their findings seem to verify the tradition as the results were consistent with known Roman road construction. There is little to see now to suggest a made way but the track is still a good fellwalker's path leading to high places. It is the one place on the fell where you are likely to meet with a fellow walker.

Fell ponies share with the ubiquitous sheep the freedom to graze peacefully on these grasslands. The red deer of Martindale recognise no boundaries and are at liberty to wander there too, but the pony is more characteristic of these quiet open spaces. This creature is a splendid sight on Loadpot's upland pastures, perhaps silhouetted against the sky where his rough, shaggy, even wild appearance belies a true docility. Quite large, he has a strength that makes him an excellent working animal and a thick, warm coat enables him to withstand the rigours of an upland winter with ease. He will browse upon the highest of the north-eastern hills in the coldest of weather.

The top of Loadpot Hill boasts a small cairn and a large O.S. column solidly constructed from colourful rock. Out of sight of the beaten track is a small, long-established cairn supporting a short flagpole. Fifty feet lower than the summit and less than a quarter of a mile to the south are the remains of a feature that once made the place unique, appearing from afar as a most unusual cairn. This was a stone fireplace complete with chimney stack, once part of the wooden shooting lodge of Lowther House. Now the chimney is no more. When last I visited the spot a small group of ponies were grazing around the remains. The stones were stretched in a neat horizontal line across the base of the former hut as though the collapse had been both recent and sudden. Remembering the wanton destruction of Robinson's Cairn on Pillar and similar acts of vandalism on Pike o'Blisco and elsewhere in recent years, one's suspicions at the cause of this fall are aroused. The Lowther House chimney stack was of no great importance but many fellwalkers will feel the loss of an eccentric landmark.

Two northern subsidiaries of Loadpot Hill are Bonscale Pike and Arthur's Pike. These are the rocky bastions that overlook the north-eastern shore of Ullswater, giving a degree of drama that acts as a foil to the more pastoral Watermillock side. There is no direct link between the two because Swarthbeck Gill cuts deeply into the intermediate hillside. Bonscale Pike has long owned two proud beacons, sited so as to be conspicuous from below. A new pillar now stands close to the well constructed Bonscale Tower, the other "stone man" being a couple of hundred yards south along the escarpment. There is a small summit cairn on one of the grassy humps that stand a short way back from the brink of the crags.

The heights of Ullswater's eastern shore seem to attract the builders of outstanding cairns and beacons. There are prominent specimens on Place Fell, but the daddy of them all sits on top of the modest hill overlooking Howtown Bay. The Hallin Fell beacon, twice as high as a man and square in plan, covers a ground area of perhaps half a dozen square yards. This must be one of the most massive summit cairns in Lakeland. Its home is one of the most straightforward summits to reach. A short, steep climb from Howtown along the Martindale road brings the low pass of The Hause underfoot, and then less than half a mile of well trodden turf is the green road to the top. There is a worthwhile view of the lower reach of the lake and Martindale is also well displayed.

Hallin Fell is the home of a memorial to one whose efforts did much to preserve the Ullswater we all know, though you will have to leave the fell to see it. Lord Birkett stood for the wishes of a great many people in his opposition to the hopes of Manchester Corporation and its thirst for water. The intention to raise the water level, by however slight an amount, would have affected the shoreline and bays and inlets would have suffered changes in shape or even loss of identity. Lord Birkett's speech in the House of Lords proved a successful plea. It was his final duty for he died soon afterwards. Our debt to his efforts is acknowledged in a most appropriate fashion where Kailpot Crag reaches into Ullswater. A tribute to his memory has been set in the rock at normal water level—it is an inscription that can only be seen from the lake.

Hallin Fell and Place Fell are well worth climbing, but for me they combine to produce one of the most delightful of all low level walks, the lakeside path between Howtown and Patterdale. From Howtown's landing stage the track sidles round Hallin Fell to Sandwick, passing through Hallin Fell Wood where nearby water twinkles between outstretched branches; in spring a scene of refreshing greens, in winter frosts a place of tinsel charm. West of Sandwick for three-quarters of a mile the way keeps above a wall enclosing pastures in pleasant but unexceptional rural surroundings. There is, however, one spot along here that I remember well. Where Scalehow Beck crosses the track after its hectic plunge down the fellside I once enjoyed a timeless summer half-hour watching some of the finest specimens of dragon-fly playing happy helicopters above quiet, shady pools.

Down by the water's edge a change of direction opens up new views. This is a feature of the walk, the constantly unfolding vistas which display further reaches of the lake. Soon comes a section where a group of names paints a picture of fairyland allure. Silver Crag, Silver Hill, Silver Point and Silver Bay hold out a promise that is entirely fulfilled. There are stands of trees framing views that linger in the memory. Patches of grass, like lawns in a landscaped garden, and bays and beaches along the shore, defy the hurried step, and when yet another headland is rounded the head of the lake is still not seen. It sometimes seems that Ullswater goes on for ever and many will wish that this were true.

From Silver Point onwards the fellside is at its steepest. They say you can find glow-worms on this flank of Place Fell, if you know where to look, and these creatures represent for me a romance fully in keeping with the charms of so beautiful a setting. Above the path are crags and scree, old workings and a disused quarry—softened by nature's greenery—and tracks draw the visitor on to destinations unseen. It is a place for quiet and careful exploration. Place Fell with its motley summits of Kilbert How, The Knight, Birk Fell, Round How and High Dodd, and its tiny nameless tarns, deserves greater fame.

Beyond Ullswater the narrowing valley reaches past Brotherswater to Kirkstone Pass, with a surround of high fells and secretive valleys. The western shore too holds much scope for the discerning walker but one fell above all captures the attentions of those who turn that way—Helvellyn must rank with Scafell Pike as a magnet for all who venture upon the fells.

Helvellyn was my first Lakeland mountain. I was led up the royal road from Grisedale, through the famous gap in the wall and along Striding Edge, then down past Grisedale Tarn to Grasmere. A high wind raced across the summit, as it always seems to do when I go that way, conjuring the stirring strains of a Wagner overture throughout the descent. From then on, as a fellwalker I was "hooked". I can never traverse Striding Edge too often. Perhaps it was at its best when swirling mists boiled out of Nethermost Cove and drifted down to Red Tarn with occasional glimpses of water, sometimes tantalisingly close, often far distant in infinite depths. The rocks of the Edge assumed unsuspected shapes and though I had crossed so many times the arête seemed delightfully longer than ever remembered so that I felt like going back to do it again—and yet again.

But Helvellyn is not just Striding Edge. As third in order of height of our mountains it is a firm favourite of the many visitors who only occasionally climb the hills. Really it is two fells in one. From the west an extensive though rather unexciting slope is largely hidden by conifers from the motorist beside Thirlmere. To the east it presents one of the most inspiring mountain scenes in the district. Complementary to the incomparable Striding Edge is Swirral Edge, across the cove of Red Tarn. This is much shorter and steeper for the cleavage of the rock is across rather than parallel to the arête as on the better known ridge. After the sharp drop from the summit plateau Swirral Edge suddenly springs to life in the form of an almost conical peak, Catstycam. There are also steep ridges leading up from the east to the subsidiary heights of Nethermost and Dollywaggon Pikes, where care is needed in desolate surroundings.

Like High Street, Helvellyn is the high point of a long ridge— a longer ridge in fact, if you just count the distance between the first and last summits to be traversed. There are perhaps thirteen walking miles from Nab Scar to Clough Head at an average altitude of over 2,500 feet and apart from the drop to Grisedale Tarn most of the way is rarely below that figure.

In common with certain other fells Helvellyn's altitude has been subject to revision in recent years. We have long believed 3,118 feet to be correct so a reduction of two feet is hard to accept, fact though it may be. There are other facts, however, that can never be denied. Striding Edge is surely the best elevated quarter mile in Lakeland, and where the track reaches the summit is a tablet in memory of the dog that guarded its master's body long after his death; on the rocks of Striding Edge is a rusty memorial to a fox hunter who fell there; and in 1926 an aeroplane landed on the summit. That it was then able to take off and fly safely away is perhaps the most startling fact of all!

8.   Keswick

KESWICK must be the finest of all centres for fellwalking. In whichever direction you face there are hills of real quality, but for the purposes of this chapter let us consider only the north. Here is an extensive region, much of which differs in character from the fell country in general, and much of which is largely unvisited. Just two fells rank high in popular esteem: Blencathra and Skiddaw. They form a curtain of high land across northern Lakeland, a screen that lends an aura of mystery to the quiet hills "back o'Skidda' ".

On the way north from Dunmail Raise the discerning traveller catches a glimpse of those sequestered heights, for the curtain is parted slightly to reveal Great Calva and the gentle skyline of Knott beyond the Glenderaterra valley. The group of fells of which they are part is circumscribed to the north, east and west by the road through Caldbeck and to the south by the valleys of Dash Beck and the river Caldew. This is no place to go in search of serrated ridges or bare peaks; nor are there tarns to gladden the eye—the outstanding exception of Bowscale Tarn is really outside this far northern area. Yet these are hills with a gentle character of their own, worth a visit if only to bring the exciting mountains of the south back into bold relief.

Highest of the group is Knott with its vast acres of tussocky grass, a confusing place should mist descend. More interesting is Great Calva whose top is crossed by a fence, an aid to navigation as it leads safely down to the Dash and Caldew valleys. The summit has the distinction of a few rocks, the source of material for a couple of cairns and a windshelter which on my last visit proved the most efficient in my memory. I was able to light a pipe despite a vigorous gale with the expenditure of a single match. Pipemen will recognise a rare and blissful moment.

Extending farthest north is High Pike, Caldbeck's beacon fell. The large, bare patch occupied by fire on important occasions has for company an O.S. column, a cairn beside an ample heap of stones, a stone memorial seat and the ruins of a cottage. High Pike's summit is certainly a place to remember but it has a rival to the east where Carrock Fell guards the north-eastern corner of Lakeland. The craggy front is a grand contrast to the rest of this otherwise slate-based range of hills. Its summit is unique, for here is the ruin of an ancient hill fort. The position of the encircling wall is clearly distinguishable as a mound of stones, continuous except for gaps coinciding with the four points of the compass, probably gateways. The wall encloses the summit cairn in an area measuring some 250 by 100 yards.

On the western fringe of this region is a feature that is unusual in the context of the surrounding sheep-walks. Separating the modest foothills of Great Cockup and Meal Fell is Trusmadoor. The easy progression of the ridge is interrupted by a relatively deep pass, a sudden groove exposing minor slaty crags on either side. As a child I saw a picture of Moses waving his staff over the Red Sea, the waters being shown parted to allow passage for the Israelites through an enormous V-shaped cleft. The abrupt gap of Trusmadoor is strangely reminiscent of that picture, though the passing flock is in the main four legged and woolly.

Sheep have their personal heaven on these slopes. I once took my lunch by Trusmadoor and watched a legion of the creatures grazing on the flank of Burn Tod across the valley. A peaceful quiet was broken when a solitary ewe voiced her satisfaction in the provender, her praise being taken up by others until a ripple of bleating spread across the fellside culminating in an echoing chorus of joy; then silence, a stillness which lasted some moments before the whole performance began again, with an endless sequence of repeats. I felt a sudden sense of comedy in the process and burst out laughing.

In comparison with these quiet hills, Blencathra is a busy mountain, though it enjoys a reputation among discriminating walkers as a place away from the motley throng. It has been known as Blencathra since mountains were first named. The more modern alternative, "Saddleback", is hard to understand unless you approach from the east from where it is as obvious a descriptive name as any in the fell country. Yet "Blencathra" is a title with strong historical foundation. Its meaning is uncertain but there is good reason to accept "Hill of Devils" for there are accounts of strange occurrences having taken place on its slopes and on the neighbouring Souther Fell.

The most reported example was in the summer of 1745 when local people swore before a magistrate that they had seen an army crossing the skyline of Souther Fell. Subsequent exploration revealed not a mark of its passing. It has been suggested that this could have been a trick of refracted light for it was learned that Prince Charles' rebel forces had been on the move in southern Scotland at precisely the same time. The fact that it took place on mid-summer eve—as did other "visions"— would lend credibility to the idea of a ghostly manifestation. In days gone by mid-summer eve was regarded with almost similar supertitious awe as Hallowe'en as an occasion for supernatural events.

The southern aspect of Blencathra can lay claim to being the most formidable mountain scene to flank a major road in England. A series of truncated spurs separated by profound ravines soars skyward, each narrowing to an arête near its top and each practicable as a route of ascent. The three spurs are bounded by a pair of rounded ridges, Blease Fell to the west and Scales Fell to the east. They resemble a couple of mighty bookends giving stability to the whole array of massive mountain structure. The enclosed spurs are, from west to east, Gategill, Hall's and Doddick Fells and the central one terminates exactly at the summit of Blencathra. As a way up this ridge has much to commend it and is as direct as could be wished. Undeniably steep, it is full of interest and becomes a true arête as height is gained. Narrow Edge it is called in these higher reaches and, though not in the same class as Striding Edge, it is narrow enough to satisfy most scramblers.

Blencathra's most famous ridge, the one all climbers make for eventually, is tucked away to the north-east. Sharp Edge, a sort of flying buttress to the summit plateau, is hidden from prying eyes. It can present a challenge to the novice walker though the problems are more apparent than real. Even the awkward step where the ridge abuts the main fell owes its reputation to its situation rather than any inherent difficulty. Ascent seems easier than descent, probably because the eyes then have the main mass of the mountain before them rather than the beckoning abyss at either side of the edge. Scales Tarn looks a long way below when nervous feet are seeking purchase on sloping slate.

The summit rests on the brink of the savage scar that is the south face. To the north a gentle grassland slopes easily to a depression beyond which is the top of Foule Crag and Sharp Edge. This is the saddle giving the fell its secondary name. An impermanent tarn is contained in the hollow and there are two crosses marked out in white stones. The larger, in view from the summit, is a memorial to a walker who suffered a fatal fall in the vicinity.

Blencathra may with some justification be called the "Fell-walker's Mountain" but among these northern fells the popular favourite is Skiddaw. It is most easily recognised from the south, with its attendant satellites a classic of composition in form and proportion. Each shapely pyramid reflects the next in a perfect build-up leading with inevitability to the Grand Old Man himself. There is no older mountain in Cumbria. Other sides display different qualities. From the west is seen a sterner face more in keeping with the Skiddaw one learns to respect on closer acquaintance. This aspect, from near the foot of Bassenthwaite Lake or better still from the low hills of Wythop, really allows you to get a truer "feel" of the mountain. Purple-grey screes below the summit ridge frown down upon Bassenthwaite, especially when surmounted by a cap of cloud. Perhaps the most surprising viewpoint is to the north or north-west from where a gentler, tamer elevation is almost unrecognisable as one of Lakeland's 3,000 foot giants, though not without a certain presence.

The most popular way up must be the tourist track from Keswick. It is a fair supposition that more visitors reach the top by this route than by all others put together. There is a good selection of alternatives for those who shun the crowds and by far the best is the splendid ridge of Ullock Pike. If it had its roots in Keswick's vale this would surely be one of the most popular ascents in the Lake Counties. Its airy roof-tree allows no variation and leads round the hidden valley of Southerndale, presided over by the bold west face of Skiddaw whose final slopes hold no comfort for gentle footed pedestrians.

The only flaw in this line of ascent is that Skiddaw Little Man can only be visited by a detour, though an alternative descent by the popular path can put this to rights. The Little Man, while necessarily subservient to the major summit, is a minor top with major claims. Is it the finest viewpoint in the land? The answer can only be a matter of opinion, but what is certain is that here is a panorama of the highest quality. The land beneath your feet slides away in a downward sweep that takes it quite out of mind. Far below the beautiful vale of Keswick brings the map in your hand to life, Newlands valley is as delectable as ever and the Jaws of Borrowdale smile a promise for the future. The backcloth is a 180 degree arc of the district's greatest mountains.

Despite its superior altitude, Skiddaw cannot compete as a point of view, but as a summit it must be given the palm. The barren, windswept ridge in the sky, perhaps half a mile in length, has its highest point about 200 yards from the northern end. Here the officers of the Ordnance Survey erected a column around which in recent years they have added a skirt of white painted stones, an aid to aerial survey, I believe. They should have known better. No stone that is not very securely cemented in place remains long unturned on so popular a summit, and they now lend a modicum of foreign decoration to the mosaic of the wall shelter, one of many which offer only token resistance to the winds that so often lash the top of England's fourth highest mountain.

Skiddaw must receive more visitors than almost any other

fell, so much so that one gets the feeling that it must be gradually wearing away. In the circumstances it comes as a surprise to note one more alteration on post-1966 O.S. maps. Dear old "Skidda'" must be smiling. After all the erosive efforts of humanity and nature its summit now stands at 3,054 feet, an extra foot nearer the sky!

9.   Coledale

THE hills lying between Derwentwater and Buttermere contain some of the best ridge walking country in the district;
a land of easy gradients and fine mountains, of minimum effort
and maximum reward. Generally, the most taxing part of any
outing is at the outset for once the ridge is gained all is plain
sailing. In this lazy fellwalker's paradise the round of the Coledale Fells stands supreme. Coledale is an unremarkable valley
with little to offer walkers except a quick way into the hills,
along the road to the old mines of Force Crag and up to Coledale
Hause. Beyond the houses of Braithwaite are three straight miles
without sign of habitation. Here all is quiet and lonely, but not
so the enclosing ridge. That is where the walkers go and with
reason, for this is one of the classic routes of Lakeland.

If the Coledale Horseshoe is taken clockwise the first target
is Causey Pike, and who could wish for a better start to a day on
the fells? The peak is a prominent and enticing object in
Keswick's outlook over Derwentwater, the terminal point of
a ridge that resembles some sleeping giant's leg at rest in the
fells with Causey Pike, the foot, thrusting five stubby toes
towards the sky. The big toe is the summit, where a pleasant
final scramble may persuade pusillanimous pedestrians to use
their hands as an aid to balance on the boot-worn track. You
certainly enjoy a sensation of being on high atop Causey Pike.
There is an abrupt slope on three sides of the turf-free top. The
view of Coledale is interrupted by the lesser elevation of Outer-
side and the delightful minor hill of Barrow, a pair of peaceful
sentinels watching over the valley and worth a couple of hours
of anyone's time. To the south is the narrow strath of Rigg Beck
where a lonely track provides for walkers a simple connection
with Buttermere.

The way west from Causey Pike can also be used as a route
to Buttermere if followed through to Whiteless Pike. This is good

47

walking country. The whale-back of Scar Crags is crossed with long, easy strides and the only dull section is the plod to the top of Sail. The grassy way is always narrow enough to allow little deviation as its aims unerringly for Eel Crag, though the track does by-pass the small cairn on Sail. Conscientious walkers always take the trouble to pay it a visit. Eel Crag is the hub of this mountain system though subservient to its western neighbour, Grasmoor, in terms of height. I suspect that despite its superior altitude the latter has fewer visitors if only because Eel Crag is a sort of Piccadilly Circus of these north-western fells. Grasmoor is in the nature of a dead end.

Eel Crag's main rock face overlooks the head of Coledale but to the south is one physical feature of real distinction. Search Lakeland as you wish but you will hardly find a better example of a hanging valley than that above the head of Sail Beck. Addacomb Hole is its name. Like a huge volcanic crater with one half sliced away, its rim bites into a wide prairie that declines west from the summit.

Eel Crag is named Crag Hill on the O.S. map, the popular name being reserved for the craggy northern end of the summit ridge. No doubt this is technically correct and it avoids confusion with a nearby namesake at the head of the Newlands valley. The Ordnance Survey seems to have a liking for renaming fells here-abouts. Three quarters of a mile south-west is Wandope (pro-nounced "Wonn-dup"), called Wanlope on modern maps. To the north is Hopegill Head, known to many a walker as Hobcarton Pike, though in this case I prefer the more exact O.S. name. Neither is strictly on Coledale's horseshoe route but if time allows I always visit them.

Wandope has little merit as a summit although 2,533 feet in height. It is only the edge of a grassy, upland plateau but it has long been a favourite of mine. On a sunny day I like to perch on the rim of the escarpment to open my lunch packet and there are comfortable enough ledges below the edge should the wind blow. The prevailing wind coming from behind then whips smartly overhead, northerly winds are deflected by high ground around Eel Crag and the best view is directly in front. What a breathtaking vista it is on one of those days when recent rain has made the peaks stand out like cardboard cut-outs in crystal air. Stretching across the landscape is range after range of hills, while the valley of Sail Beck far beneath one's feet brings an element of depth to the scene. From Ard Crags and Knott Rigg to the distant climax of Helvellyn and the Dodds I have counted seven ridges in all, some quite small in stature but so perfectly pro-portioned that it needs little imagination to believe oneself in one of those remote mountain regions of which the humble fellwalker often dreams. Incline your head to the south and the drama of a distant Scafell skyline is yours to enjoy. Nearer to hand the pride of the Buttermere fells completes an outstanding panorama.

The next summit of the Coledale Horseshoe is Grisedale Pike, but only a short diversion is necessary to include Hopegill Head. It is a detour that should not be omitted. The top, where rock breaks through the grassy tegument of these ridges, can only be a few square yards in area but, fine though this platform is, the situation and approaches are what give real character to the peak. It stands exactly at the meeting point of three fine ridges, leading from Whiteside, Ladyside Pike and Grisedale Pike, while to the north-east and plunging from the very summit is the formidable precipice of Hobcarton Crag.

The final approach from Ladyside Pike is particularly good, being over gently angled bare rock. This is a hazard in icy conditions and a careless step could bring a sudden and unpremeditated study of the details of Hobcarton Crag—or a sharp descent into the confines of Hope Gill, the valley at whose head the summit lies. The only disappointing feature of this splendid mountain is the dull southern flank which slopes gently to Coledale Hause, interrupted merely by the rounded bulge of Sand Hill.

Grisedale Pike is the final height on this round. It is named after Grisedale Gill which drains north-east towards Bassenthwaite Lake, but the mountain occupies the northern wall of Coledale throughout its length. After Eel Crag this is the highest point on the route, the culmination of the pyramid that is well seen from Keswick. These fells have the same slate base as the Skiddaw group, the material being responsible for the generally smooth slopes and easy ridges. On the summit of Grisedale Pike the rock is obvious underfoot and it exists in plenty as long runs of scree on the Coledale flank. It is not the stuff of which grand cairns are made; it is too friable to provide useful pieces, though on my last visit a tall and delicate specimen stood on the rock platform that is the highest point. Whether it retained its fine proportions for long is open to doubt. I would like to hope so for this is a shapely mountain and deserves such recognition.

10. Borrowdale

Grange Fell — Rosthwaite Fell — Glaramara — High Spy — Catbells.

IF a poll were taken in which all interested parties were asked to nominate their favourite valley it is likely that Borrowdale would prove the popular choice. The blend of tree, grass, water and rock is exquisitely mingled and wherever man has touched the scene he has added to it; each wall, house and bridge seems to have grown into the landscape as surely as the trees, and signs of industry are expertly masked by nature's sylvan greenery. This valley has something for all and this very fact is its undoing. Go there in the holiday season and it would seem that everyone is there. You must climb the fells to stand a chance of escaping the crowds and even so you will not be alone. Choose a quiet, off-season day for exploring Borrowdale.

The first village of the dale is Grange, beyond which the Jaws of Borrowdale tighten on the valley's lifeline. There is barely enough room for the road to squeeze through beside the river and I suppose this is one of the places that the poet Gray negotiated fearful that any undue noise might bring an avalanche crashing about his ears. The enclosing heights of Castle Crag and King's How do their unsuccessful best to seal the valley from the outside world.

King's How is National Trust property, purchased and named in memory of King Edward VII, and no sovereign could have a better memorial than this jewel among Lakeland's smaller hills. It is a minor summit of Grange Fell—Brund Fell is the highest point—but King's How deserves designation as the summit supreme. It is a superb station for viewing the geography of upper Borrowdale, a green basin whose pattern of fields displays a harmony not always present when man leaves his mark on the scene. All round is some of Lakeland's loveliest scenery and beyond is an array of mountains, each a magnet in its own right but none with a summit as conducive to a prolonged halt as this. No one ever hurries on Grange Fell.

50

Brund Fell lies to the south-east of King's How. It proclaims its superior altitude by bristling with chunks of rock both large and small, a scrambler's paradise. The well used Rosthwaite/ Watendlath track is a further half mile distant, skirting the southern limit of Grange Fell. Beyond is Great Crag, a less known eminence but with an attractive flank facing Borrowdale and the side valley of Stonethwaite.

The slopes across Stonethwaite are a springboard to the highest land in the country. The Scafell range is much more extensive than many realise and the north ridge has its logical termination here at the foot of Rosthwaite Fell, five miles from the summit of the Pike as that black baron of the fells, the raven, flies. Rosthwaite Fell has one of the quietest tops in Borrowdale, which is not surprising with so much good walking country in the vicinity. The fell suffers in comparison with its neighbours and is often dismissed as a marshy wilderness. Certainly there is much wet ground amid the hillocks of its widespread and largely pathless ridge, but other hills of similar character have their admirers. It is unfortunate that there is no well defined summit on Rosthwaite Fell. The best nominee would be Bessyboot were there not higher land three-quarters of a mile further south, beyond the curiously named Tarn at Leaves. Even that is upstaged by the lower rocky tor of Rosthwaite Cam. This has a look of impregnability from certain angles though its tiny cairn can be reached without difficulty. The limits of Rosthwaite Fell are defined on the west by Comb Gill, above which is the hill's most notable feature—Doves Nest Caves. These, the best known natural caves in the district, have been formed by a landslip. A large section of crag seems to have moved forward and downward to leave dark and grimy gaps for the expert to explore. Comb Gill is otherwise an unremarkable valley, but it does offer an easy line of ascent to the Rosthwaite Fell/Glaramara ridge by way of Comb Door.

Glaramara is one of my favourite mountain names. The list seems to grow in contemplation; names that roll smoothly from the tongue, each evoking memories of days on the hills. Days of mist or rain, days of sun, wind or snow, each with its own pleasures and pains but none regretted. Mist on Blencathra and Great Gable, Pillar in the rain, an ever smiling sun on Haystacks, Helvellyn's gales—and the first snows of winter on Glaramara. You can spend a lot of time with such thoughts on Lakeland's tops and Glaramara provides as much opportunity as most hills when the weather is right to allow a quiet, contemplative pipe, whether on the summit or in the priceless setting of one of the delightful diminutive tarns.

If you reach Glaramara from Rosthwaite Fell you will find an immediate improvement in the track, now well marked and cairned. After visiting the double summit this path meanders along the ridge to Esk Hause, passing on the way one of my favourite mountain tarns. I can think of none better of like size. This, tiny and nameless on my map though sometimes called Lincomb Tarn, rests in a cradle of rock just beyond High House Tarn on the journey south. Probably the title Lincomb Tarns— in the plural—should really be applied to a small group of tarns hereabouts, but as I like the name almost as much as the tarn I shall go on using it, even if in error. The ridge in the neighbourhood is particularly well favoured in the provision of rocky pools, although the tiny mere in question is unmistakable. The backdrop is a rocky curtain which plunges sheer into the water, but the pool is sufficiently open to the sky to reflect the slightest change in mood of the weather. Lincomb Tarn is in miniature my ideal of the perfect mountain tarn.

West of the main Borrowdale valley is a continuous wall of rough fell breached by the occasional ravine. The lack of marked summits after the initial upthrust of Catbells means that the uninitiated tend to by-pass this area and head for obvious heights elsewhere. The spine lies well back and overlooks the Newlands valley rather than Borrowdale. It is in fact a good and well loved ridge with a splendid track, typical of the north-western fell country. The highest point is a mile west of Castle Crag. It enjoys the graphic name of High Spy and owns various aliases, including Eel Crags though this really refers to the rocky ramparts defending the ridge on the Newlands side. The most obvious way up from Borrowdale uses the old road to Rigghead's disused quarries and takes walkers into the recesses of Tongue Gill. A good start is from Grange where the old road begins, opposite the church. A merit of this route is that a short detour allows a visit to the top of Castle Crag for a detailed view of mid-Borrowdale, with the flat valley floor that was the bed of a lake in ancient times.

This easily graded way is the first stage of an excellent route which can return the walker to Grange after a traverse of the ridge over Maiden Moor to Catbells. After High Spy is left behind all is plain sailing with a gentle downward gradient almost all the way. On the left are glimpses of Newlands' upper valley between the battlements of Eel Crags and all the time there is being unfolded the panorama of the vale of Keswick, with Derwentwater springing fully into view at Blea Crag. A slight deviation to the right to visit the cairn thereon brings excellent rewards.

The first and last fell of Borrowdale is Catbells. It may be only 1,481 feet in height but there is no denying its challenging outline. It has the shape of a mountain, a shape that attracts anyone with a feeling for high places, and there must be many

A dramatic view of the famous Striding Edge, Helvellyn (chapter 7).

Panorama from Sail looking over Causey Pike, Rowling End being submerged in mist along with Keswick and Derwentwater. The Pennines are visible in the far distance (chapter 9).

Walkers on Sharp Edge en route for the summit of Blencathra (chapter 8).

The Borrowdale fells of Maiden Moor and High Crags as seen from Rowling End (chapter 10).

An aerial view of the western fells looking towards Buttermere. Great Gable is on the near right (chapter 11).

The Ennerdale fells from Green Gable (chapter 12).

A fell-walker pauses to look at Scafell and Scafell Pike (chapter 13).

folk who first felt the urge to take up fellwalking after an initial glance across Derwentwater from Keswick. Despite its position at the end of a ridge it manages to convey the impression of isolation and anyone on the summit experiences the sensation of being on a solitary hill. This is a feeling so often absent on higher fells where the top may be buttressed on most sides by high land, effectively eliminating depth from the view.

From Catbells the view is uncompromisingly down for almost a thousand feet, except to the south where the connecting ridge lies. To the east Derwentwater is supreme, its scatter of islands bringing out the Robinson Crusoe that lurks in the hearts of all embryo explorers, and toytown vessels ply upon the waters weaving a pattern of wakes across a fairyland sea. Keswick is a mystic eastern city, its harsher outlines softened by a dressing of leafy greenery. Turn round and you see a different design. The fields of Newlands hold a pastoral tranquillity that helps to make this one of the most placidly beautiful of all valleys. Closing the dale is the mysterious and forbidden little hill of Swinside. Resting like a football on the penalty spot, waiting for the boot of Catbells to shoot it through the goalmouth formed by Grisedale Pike and Skiddaw, it leads the eye over Bassenthwaite Lake to the hazy coastal plain of the Solway Firth.

Beyond this prospect of valleys is a backcloth of mountains, viewed in their true perspective from this moderate elevation. There is none of the foreshortening that is inevitable from a valley, yet you are below the tops of most of the surrounding fells so that they do not suffer in stature when compared with your viewpoint. You see them as they really are. To me Catbells is a fell for a morning stroll, so that the exquisite outlook can be enjoyed before being blurred by the hazy heat of a warm summer day. If you make this delectable little hill your destination you will enjoy rewards quite out of proportion with the modest effort expended in its ascent.

11.   Buttermere

IT was late July and possibly the finest day of a superb summer.
Our journey up Buttermere's valley was brought to a pre-
mature halt below Grasmoor as the first wide expanse of Crummock Water came into view. No ripple disturbed the surface and
the fell opposite—Mellbreak—cast a perfect inverted image upon
the waters. Our group was not without cameras but no one had
the presence of mind to take a photograph; the scene was so
hypnotic that it seemed sufficient just to stand and stare. Perhaps
it is as well. The result would surely have provoked the
argument: "Which is up and which is down?" This was almost
typical of the Buttermere of my experience. Of course the dale
does have its share of the district's wettest weather but for me
it is the Sunshine Valley. Even in late October I have sat for a
couple of hours in shirt sleeves on a Buttermere summit, soaking
up the late autumn sunshine and reading from a selection of
Sunday papers that my companion had unexpectedly hauled
from his ruc-sac.

Grasmoor is Buttermere's highest mountain and a fiercely
imposing object it is when seen from near the foot of the valley,
after rounding the initial screen of Whiteside. There is a common
misconception that Grasmoor takes its name from the most
obvious characteristic of its broad summit plateau, very much
a grassy moorland. Indeed there is a tendency to mis-spell the
name by including a second "s", but this title has its roots in the
word "grise" meaning wild boar. No one is likely to think of grass
when looking at the fell from the foot of Crummock Water.
These crags are quite untypical of a mainly slate mountain. Nor
does vegetation come to mind when viewing the south face from
neighbouring Whiteless Pike. That unremitting slope of finely
shattered scree must be just about the least frequented spot in
Lakeland.

Whiteless Pike is a true pike in appearance when viewed from the west. The track to the summit is well marked, as might be expected with such an obvious way to the heights. It is quite steep in its upper reaches where a series of zig-zags brings the climber to a small and airy top. The Pike is really the high point of a ridge rising from the wide hillside of Whiteless Breast, a grassy alp from where the final tower beckons temptingly. Beyond the summit the track continues along a splendid rooftop ridge to Thirdgill Head Man, with Third Gill below on the right and Rannerdale Beck down to the left. This is the first stage of the high road to Newlands, a quality mountain crossing where the walker remains on high all the way to Causey Pike.

These fells and others north of Buttermere are excellent objectives for the fellwalker but they are not directly connected, except for the final trio of Robinson, Hindscarth and Dale Head, and the latter is really a Newlands fell. That is the dale at the head of which it lies. Across the valley is a different lay-out, one of the finest and most highly regarded ridge walks in Cumbria. Red Pike is the first of the Buttermere triunity that most attracts walkers who enter the valley. The companion members are High Stile and High Crag, though the traverse of the ridge can be extended in either direction by the inclusion of Great Borne and Starling Dodd to the west and Haystacks to the east.

Red Pike has a Wasdale namesake. Both are fells of character though their appeal is different. The Wasdale fell has my preference as a fellwalker's mountain but Buttermere's Red Pike is undeniably the more deserving of the name. Its summit is more pronounced, as befits a fell bearing the title "pike", and the justification of the adjective is there for all to see. Red it is indeed, the colouring being due to the presence of syenite in the soil. The usual line of ascent, whose popularity is excruciatingly apparent when underfoot, is the track through Burtness Wood to Bleaberry Tarn. There are other ways to and from the summit, some steep, but none more laborious than this. An important claim of Red Pike is part ownership of Lakeland's highest waterfall. Scale Force is on the boundary stream dividing the fell from neighbouring Starling Dodd.

The central peak of the Buttermere threesome is High Stile and the time to be at the top is late afternoon when all is quiet and the sun is in the west. Here is a study in depth. The abrupt plunge of Chapel Crags allows no foreground to the view and almost a thousand feet below is Bleaberry Comb with its tarn, the only impediment to the gaze as it focuses on the village. This fairyland hamlet seems near enough for a lobbed pebble to disturb the equanimity of an elfin population. Beyond Red Pike's minor protégé of Dodd, Crummock Water points the eye to the pleasantly pastoral Vale of Lorton. At first glance the valley seems to have only one lake, but a corner of Buttermere does peep into view around the edge of High Stile's north-eastern spur.

High Stile has two splendid corries. Bleaberry Comb is well known to walkers but Burtness (or Birkness) Comb is frequented mainly by the rock climbing fraternity, though the occasional curious pedestrian does wander in to be rewarded by the sight of some first class rock scenery. Eagle Crag is outstanding and the finest section of the Buttermere Ridge is silhouetted against the sky. Narrow, rugged and airy, with fine views all round, it commands a frequent return. The depths of Burtness Comb on the one hand are contrasted with the more mundane Ennerdale slope; yet that side also holds excitement for observant eyes if the lighting is right. Over there beyond the works of the Forestry Commission is another crenellated wall, a land of crag and corrie to duplicate the dramas of Buttermere.

At the end of the Buttermere Ridge is High Crag, a mountain of bold proportions when viewed from the valley. To a wanderer coming off Haystacks with the intention of continuing in this direction the appearance can be positively forbidding. This eastern face, Gamlin End, is rough and abounds in scree. The only partial breach in the stony defences is a steep grass slope which merges with the scree well below the summit. In it is a series of gargantuan steps moulded by countless boots, guaranteed to test leg and thigh muscles to the limit. The descent holds little allure either, so whichever way the ridge is taken expect High Crag to make its presence felt. Even so, the summit has views to rival any on the High Stile range; any agonies are not suffered in vain.

The last fell before the valley head is Haystacks. It is a fell of contrasts. Darkly shadowed crags turn a grimly austere face to Buttermere, yet the summit acres are clothed by nature in a raiment of pleasant hues and textures. Given the right day and season this is a place for carefree wandering, when the gentle hum of industrious insects and the sparkle of standing water make it one of the most enchanting places imaginable.

If Buttermere is the Sunshine Valley then Haystacks is my Sunshine Fell. The worst weather I have suffered there has been a stiff breeze and even that was tempered by the sun's rays. Of course, I have chosen my days well. The fell can only be appreciated to the full on a day when true summer slows the pace and time is of no consequence. There are memories of lunches on rocky outcrops by the shore of Innominate Tarn with the summit lying beyond the water, patiently waiting for lazy footsteps to take us that way. Gentle strolls through sundrenched heather have been accompanied by the serenade of assiduous bees gathering a rich harvest of Haystacks' special honey. An eventual arrival at the summit rocks, the cradle of a delightful rock-pool tarn, has brought once more that view of Buttermere with Gatesgarth's distant buildings a set of tiny dolls' houses in a bower of trees. Haystacks is the epitome of Lakeland's choicest offerings and for many is the finest fell of all.

1 .   Ennerdale

ENNERDALE must be the least visited of the major valleys. It is remote from the main tourist centres but really the Forestry Commission must take the blame for the neglect. This is a closed valley except to travellers on foot and not everyone enjoys walking under a cloak of evergreens. However, this is in some ways an asset. If you wish to escape the holiday crowds Ennerdale provides an excellent opportunity.

Because of Ennerdale's seclusion its fells are more usually ascended from other sides. In the case of the north bounding fells this would probably be the case if the valley were popular; they turn their faces to Buttermere. Yet at the western end of the ridge is one fell that should belong to Ennerdale. This is Great Borne, alternatively known as Herdus. Minor crags to the north overlook Floutern Tarn and the Ennerdale slopes are quite rough in the region of Herdus Scaw. The ridge is extensively flat and featureless west of the summit and to the east is smooth walking territory with only a grassy depression in the way of a walker bound for Starling Dodd and the Buttermere fells. Great Borne has a double top, the fractionally lower one to the north being the site of a massive cairn quite out of keeping with the importance of the hill as a fellwalking attraction. The builders knew what they were doing, however, for it is a grand spot, amply provided with cosy couches among the grassy undulations of the summit area. It is a good place to end a mountain day where, with your back against a suitable support, you can watch the large red football of the sun roll slowly out of play beyond the western sky.

The best of Ennerdale, however, lies across the lake and as you approach the dale head the mountain scenery assumes an aspect of real magnificence. The first major peak is Haycock. Largely unknown, this is 2,618 feet of forgotten fell. It stands a long way back from Wasdale and is remote enough from the Pillar Round to be left out on a limb. Nevertheless it is a rugged eminence with a summit that in some ways duplicates that of nearby Scoat Fell, crossed by a wall and decorated with stones. The upper reaches have the appearance of an upturned basin from some quarters, yet the final slopes are made aggressive by rashes of boulders. If it were within easy reach of a valley road Haycock would deservedly see many more visitors, but the long approaches guarantee a quiet day for those who seek solitude in scenery characteristic of the best in the Lake District.

Turn west from Haycock and you face some of the most exciting terrain in the land. Scoat Fell, Steeple and Pillar are part of the Pillar Round, which follows the Mosedale watershed from Black Sail Pass to Red Pike and Yewbarrow. If Kirk Fell is included this becomes the Mosedale Horseshoe, one of the great classic routes of Lakeland. It is a Wasdale walk and there is nothing better in the fellwalker's itinerary. Mosedale, the major branch valley at the head of Wasdale, provides the most usual line of approach to these fells and it is rare for one to be visited in isolation. If omissions are made the sufferers are likely to be Scoat Fell and Steeple. A well marked track by-passing Scoat Fell's summit on the Mosedale side proclaims the fact that many folk give it a miss. Not much offered there they think, but what Scoat Fell lacks may be found in plenty only a quarter of a mile to the north.

Steeple is subservient in altitude and mass to its parent fell, but in nothing else. The connecting ridge is short and leads to a lofty pinnacle, a true summit poised on the brink of space. Woe betide anyone who tries to circle the cairn. It rests on the rim of a profound gulf lined uncompromisingly with crags. Down there the wilderness of Mirk Cove and Windgap Cove attracts only those who seek the solitude of really wild and lonely places. The other flank is a gentler slope but the summit breathes the true excitement of the peaks.

Scoat Fell lives on the reflected glory of Steeple and the excellence of the coves to the north. There is an inconsistency in O.S. maps with regard to the summit contours of this fell. The one inch map proclaims a subsidiary summit about half a mile along the west ridge where a 2,750 foot contour encloses a considerable area, much greater than the true top which reaches 2,760 feet, and there would appear to be little to choose between them in altitude. A depression at about 2,630 feet is marked on the intervening ground. The 2½ inch map, which shows the ridge continuing level at this height, is more to be trusted. There are three Scoat Fells in fact. The western one is Great Scoat Fell—though most extensive it is decidedly lower than the one inch map suggests. To the east, overlooking Mosedale, is Scoat Fell. The highest point, of which there is no doubt in the mind of the walker on the spot, is the centrally placed Little Scoat Fell. The barren, stony top is distinguished by a wall, part of a boundary fence that once approximately defined the whole of the Ennerdale watershed.

Of course Pillar is the Ennerdale fell par excellence. It is a much under-rated mountain, mainly because it turns its back towards the majority of visitors. To appreciate Pillar you must see its northern face and scramble into its hidden recesses, which for most walkers means a traverse of the High Level Route from Looking Stead to Pillar Rock. The first time I explored this exciting way nebulous arms of mist reached down from darkly impending buttresses and a fine drizzle accompanied us along a vestigial track. When we reached the Rock we felt rather than saw its presence and memories are mainly of the drip, drip of water all around. A couple of years passed before I again stood by Robinson's Cairn and witnessed the reality of Pillar Rock for the first time.

There is nothing in Lakeland—or England—like it. Even Scafell's massive sculpture does not provide this kind of vertiginous spectacle because it rises from the relatively enclosed amphitheatre of Hollow Stones. The view there is either down or up, depending upon whether you are above or below the crag, whereas from Robinson's Cairn you have both in the same glance. Above soars that Rock, almost a thousand feet from its remote summit to a base broadly balanced above a further thousand foot sweep of craggy hillside, at the bottom of which Ennerdale's much castigated conifers have an insignificance only realised from here. Pillar Rock is the preserve of the rock climber. The summit is a place where none but the expert should venture, though that Muhammad Ali of fellsmen, Steeple Jackson, had his own ideas about what constitutes expertise. Like the showman of the boxing ring the Rev. James Jackson was never above proclaiming his own prowess, often in verse. After repairing the steeple of his own church he wrote:—

> *Who has not heard of Steeple Jack,*
> *That lion-hearted Saxon?*
> *Though I am not he, he was my sire,*
> *For I am Steeple Jackson.*

In 1875, aged 79, he climbed the Rock and repeated his exploit the following year. But in 1878 he was killed when he set out on his third venture to the pinnacle of his aspirations.

On our first visit we had thought that the Rock marked the limit of exploration for all but the cragsman, but not so. A scree run beyond Robinson's Cairn can be negotiated to reach a rocky terrace above the sheer plunge of the Sham Rock. At the end of the terrace a choice of rock slab or a less exposed short gully leads to a track passing an ominous stretcher box and on to the back of Pillar Rock. A steep but simple scramble then brings the summit of Pillar Mountain underfoot. An exciting route this, perhaps a little heady initially, but quite within the reach of a strong walker. Anyone who can reach Robinson's Cairn should be able to manage the rest.

Robinson's Cairn was erected by members of the Fell and Rock Climbing Club in memory of John Wilson Robinson, a well known local fellsman who died in 1907. This lover of the fells showed interest in the development of Pillar Rock as a climbing ground. His cairn is admirably situated both as a viewpoint for the Rock and as a target for those following the High Level Route. Unfortunately it has also proved a target for a less desirable element whose presence the fells could well do without. Its destruction in 1973 can only be deplored and rebuilding, no matter how well executed, does not remove the distaste that such vandalism inevitably leaves in its wake.

John Wilson Robinson is said to have scaled Pillar Rock over a hundred times. How often he stood on top of Pillar Mountain I do not know. The summit is an anticlimax, large, flat and spacious, but a superb viewpoint. It was one of my earliest achievements in the fells. We reached it on a crisp, clear sunny day in late October and spent a considerable time savouring the circumjacent summits which reach out in a ripple of ridges to farthest Lakeland. The distant sheen of a satin sea helped to create a sense of isolation, leaving us alone in a benevolent universe. From that time on Pillar has ranked as one of my top favourites among Lakeland's fells.

13.   Wasdale

THE portals of Wasdale are dominated by The Screes. It is impossible to enter the valley without being aware of that wide-screen presence beyond England's deepest lake. Impressive enough in all conditions, this is one of the most vivid mountain scenes in the country if the time and season are right. I remember leaving Wasdale late one October, the sun's autumn disc low in the sky ahead. We stopped near the foot of the lake to take a last look at the mountain family grouped at the valley head but our gaze was arrested before ever reaching Great Gable and company. The Screes held the stage.

How can a screen of mere stone display such colour? Dying brackens helped to set alight the patterned fans of debris as late afternoon sunshine brought its spotlight to bear. For perhaps ten minutes we looked as the magnificence faded and twilight's shadows took command. Evening light seems to bring out something special in this scene, but The Screes have a quality of their own—a quality of drama if not always of beauty that is discernible at any season. I doubt if there is a more impressive sight in England for the motorist. The Screes represent as large an expanse of rock as he is likely to see anywhere in the country. Admittedly much of it is in relatively small pieces, though some of those pieces are small only in relation to the mountainside. They would dwarf many a house as closer inspection will show. The average tourist would shudder at the very idea of walking there, across Wastwater amid that tumultuous display, but there is a track along that far shore and apart from two or three hundred yards of really awkward boulders near the foot of the lake the way is reasonably simple and straightforward.

For many The Screes is the whole mountain but that plunging waste of stone is only a front. In fact there are two summits, high points at either end of a wide ridge—Whin Rigg nearer the entrance to the valley and the higher Illgill Head. These are the real, though little recognised names of the fell. In the depression between them are two small tarns, shallow peaty pools which no doubt cease to exist in conditions of drought. This then is the introduction to Wasdale, two minor fells whose real glory is all in the shopwindow, there for all to see. Travel up the valley, however, and you enter a circle of truly great mountains, a land where a pair of boots is necessary to bring the mountain secrets into view.

Wasdale Head is surrounded by fells steeped in an aura of mountaineering history, many of whose names are known to folk who have no aspirations to scale the heights, fells whose names beckon with romantic attraction to adventurous beings. Scafell and The Pikes, supreme in height: Pillar and Steeple whose titles savour of the seemingly inaccessible and are more often reached from here than from Ennerdale; and of course Gable—Great Gable in fact, but affectionately known as Gable by so many walkers. Its nearby cousin is the one that needs an adjective before its name, but then Green Gable is the poor relation.

Great Gable really does seem to be Wasdale's fell. It has one foot firmly planted in the valley, and though another is directed towards Ennerdale that valley cannot present the classic mountain picture. From Wastwater the fell looks exactly as every schoolboy imagines a mountain should, the centrepiece of a superb mountain group. Not for nothing is this the scene chosen as the Lake District National Park emblem. The combination of lake and mountain embodies the ideal of Lakeland to so many people. It by no means conveys the full range of the district's attractions though so much is there in essence.

Above all Great Gable is a mountain of challenge. There can be few fellwalkers who have not early in their mountain apprenticeship faced that challenge and ventured upon Gable's stony wastes. The mountain is girdled by a ring of crags and scree. The Ennerdale side is dominated by the huge dark mass of Gable Crag. Frowning down upon Wasdale is the famed climbing ground of the Great Napes, above which the summit throws out a further defence in the form of Westmorland Crags. Between these main precipices are others, lesser only in the face of such unanswerable superiority. Where no solid rock bars the way torrents of shifting stone do their utmost to deter would be visitors to the summit. There is no easy, grassy rake to provide a simple way to the top for those of tender foot. This is a dry mountain. There is little vegetation, nor much soil to maintain it, and therefore rain quickly drains away. The only watercourses are those marking the limits of the fell. A criticism of Gable is that it has no tarn, but surely it merits part ownership of the gem at Sty Head? There are also two small ones at Beck Head, shared with Kirk Fell.

Beck Head is the half-way point of the Gable Girdle, an undeniably worthwhile walk. It takes the mere pedestrian into the heart of rock climbing country, below the crags of Kern Knotts, the Great Napes and White Napes and, beyond Beck Head, along the base of Gable Crag. At the Great Napes an upward diversion can place even the timid walker—if he takes care—on the well named platform of the Dress Circle. This ledge is the classic station for observing the pinnacle of Napes Needle and any activities taking place there. First climbed in 1886 by the legendary W. P. Haskett Smith, this must be the most famous chunk of rock in Britain. The ascent of Napes Needle seems to me almost reminiscent of the Indian rope trick. The climber arrives on the topmost block and nonchalantly stands upright, surrounded by volumes of space. Descent is so much of an anticlimax that it would not seem out of place if he were to take a bow and perform the ultimate illusion.

The summit of Great Gable, together with that of Great End and the surrounding high land, has been dedicated as a war memorial to members of the Rock and Fell Climbing Club who died fighting for their country. A bronze plaque affixed to the highest rocks is testimony to their memory. The uninitiated may think it strange that an inhospitable place like this should be held in high regard by so many sensible folk, but such is its hold on the affections of those concerned that had they the choice they would wish no finer memorial.

Some hundred yards south-west of the highest point, above the face of Westmorland Crags, is the Westmorland Cairn. Built by the brothers Westmorland in 1876 to mark a view that they considered unsurpassed by any from an English mountain, it must have witnessed the expenditure of untold reels of film in the subsequent years. The mosaic fields of Wasdale Head backed by the deepest of our lakes combine to polarise attention, but the layout of the Wasdale fells is also there to behold. To the right of the lake is the superb Yewbarrow, among the finest of little mountains, and beyond are Middle Fell and Seatallan. The latter sweeps down to the fierce front of Buckbarrow, a minor mirror of The Screes across the dale. Nearer to hand is Kirk Fell, completely overshadowed by the imperious rivalry of its magnificent neighbour. These are all splendid fells but it is their misfortune to share a valley with greater mountains. South of the Westmorland Cairn is the most fascinating fell country in the land.

The attainment of the summit of Scafell Pike affords a little extra in the way of satisfaction. Its superior altitude is sufficient attraction on a first visit but with greater knowledge comes the realisation that it is in the variety of scope for exploration that much of the merit of England's premier mountain lies. The Pike's importance as a supreme objective tends to obscure the fact that it is also the highest point of a considerable group of fells, a group with a geographical entity of its own. The range has roots in the surprisingly distant regions of Borrowdale and Eskdale, and to travel from one end to the other by road means a journey of almost fifty miles. This is one of the most unequivocal mountain barriers in the Kingdom, but for the fellwalker it is Mecca.

The finest of popular approaches involves the Corridor Route. There are a number of mountainside traverses that take the mere walker into truly mountainous surroundings. Often they were pioneered by and are the domain of the rock climber. The climber's traverse on Bowfell, the Gable Girdle and the High Level Route to Pillar Rock are three outstanding specimens, but the Corridor Route is the supreme example of its kind. It is predominantly a walker's way, devoid of technical difficulties but leading into the heart of superb rock scenery. Logically it terminates below the vast crags that frame the Mickledore gap on the Wasdale side, but as a popular route to the summit of England it has no peer. This flank also boasts the most prodigious ravine in the Lake Counties. Piers Gill bites deeply into the fell as though some long forgotten cataclysm has tried to sever bold Lingmell from the main mountain group. It reaches up to where the merry multitude cross the well defined col that is their final landmark before the prime objective—just after they have passed two related summits that would be worth a brief inspection.

Broad Crag and Ill Crag are near the well beaten tourist way, but though both are circled by a 3,000 foot contour—a rare qualification in England—you are unlikely to see anyone there. In the case of Broad Crag this is hardly surprising. Though only a stone's throw from the track its defence of chaotic boulders is enough to scare away all but the most ardent of peak baggers. It has been called with justification the roughest summit in England and any visitors will see little reason to contest that opinion. Ill Crag is slightly further from the main thoroughfare but is easier to reach. South of the small cairn is an immediate fall of savage stones with the wild valley of Little Narrowcove far below. This is the loneliest side of Scafell Pike, where remote and desolate upper Eskdale makes its final drive for Esk Hause. Rare indeed is it to see anyone down there. The only track to enjoy frequent use leaves Eskdale lower down to head for Mickledore by way of Cam Spout. This is the region of Scafell Pike's greatest secrets, a place for pioneers with inquiring minds and bold determination.

The summit of Scafell Pike is the one place above all others where there is no excuse for lack of cairns. The material for their construction is present in profusion, as the feet of all newcomers will testify, but the pile up there is really too big to be called a cairn. This massive edifice is almost a mini-mountain in itself and on summer days is festooned with the perspiring bodies of tourists contemplating the inevitable trials of the return to Langdale, Borrowdale or Wasdale. The stones have been used in the past to build shelters too, the remains being curious additions to the immediate surroundings. A unique feature of the Pike is the highest Lakeland tarn, about a quarter of a mile from the summit in the direction of Scafell. Broadcrag Tarn has no connection with the Broad Crag already mentioned—it is named from the Broad Crags overlooking the Cam Spout approach to Mickledore. Only a minority of visitors take the trouble to seek it out.

Mickledore is the Scafell system's most distinctive feature. It grants an individuality to both Scafell and Scafell Pike that could never be as marked if the traverse between the two was merely a replica of the boulder fields stretching north-east from the Pike to Great End. Mickledore originated as an intrusion of molten rock which when solidified was softer than the adjacent strata so that weathering has tended to remove the igneous material more readily. The result is the tremendous gap in the ridge and the mightiest wall of perpendicular rock in England.

The contrast between these north and east facing cliffs and the opposite side of Scafell is startling. Look at the mountain from Burnmoor Tarn and you see a rather drab slope with no suggestion of the magnificent display of rocky extravagance beyond the skyline. The first time I climbed on the Scafell group was when we set out from this gentler side of Scafell and I have always been convinced that this was a fortunate choice for a first foray on the range. The sudden revelation of Mickledore was even wilder than we had dreamed, and the more impressive for that reason.

The day unfolded like a great symphony. The opening movement began modestly with the long ascent of Green How, but increased in eventfulness as the developing north face gradually allowed tantalising peeps towards the great basin of Hollow Stones. The climax was a glance into the then unknown mysteries of Deep Gill, one key to the traverse to Scafell Pike for those who know the West Wall Traverse and Lord's Rake. The second movement was a scherzo. We set off along the apparently straight line to the Pike, playing yo-yos on the steep descent to Broad Stand. The fun and games of this episode ended when we decided we were out of our depth and returned to the summit to find our way to Mickledore via Foxes Tarn, the tiny pool that is second in height to Broadcrag Tarn.

There followed a short period of determined progress as we

made our way to the top of the Pike, intent on making up for time lost. It was happy progress, however, and this is evident in a photograph taken on the occasion; a quartet of windswept wanderers occupy the summit platform with what they hope is the panache of veteran Himalayan explorers. This really was a memorable day with a finale of increasing tempo as we made a direct descent to Wasdale Head over the shoulder of Lingmell, almost tumbling down the steep flank to Lingmell Beck.

Scafell and its Pike are big mountains, fells of great character, and whether the summits are reached by one of the popular routes or by some less trodden way there is always something of worth to enjoy. A fully committed fellwalker will not reject the old and tried approaches—here or on any fell in the district. He would be blind indeed if he could not find something new in the scenes of earlier walks. But he would surely be lacking in imagination if he did not seek out new ground, for only by so doing can he come near to a full understanding of any mountain and the Scafell range is the one above all others to keep its secrets from the common gaze. He who searches will extend not only his knowledge of England's finest mountain group. He will come closer, if only subconsciously, to an understanding of his own motivation as a fellwalker.